Maine Bucket List Adventure Guide

*Explore 100 Offbeat
Destinations You Must Visit!*

Shirley Gonzalez

Canyon Press
canyon@purplelink.org

Please consider writing a review!
Just visit: purplelink.org/review

ISBN: 978-1-957590-18-9

FREE BONUS

Discover 31 Incredible Places You Can Visit Next! Just Go To:

purplelink.org/travel

Table of Contents:

How to Use This Book

Welcome to your very own adventure guide to exploring the many wonders of the state of Maine. Not only does this book offer the most wonderful places to visit and sights to see in the vast state, but it provides GPS coordinates for Google Maps to make exploring that much easier.

Adventure Guide
Sorted by region, this guide offers over 100 amazing wonders found in Maine for you to see and explore. They can be visited in any order and this book will help you keep track of where you've been and where to look forward to going next. Each section describes the area or place, what to look for, Physical Address, and what you may need to bring along.

GPS Coordinates
As you can imagine, not all of the locations in this book have a physical address. Fortunately, some of our listed wonders are either located within a National Park or Reserve, or near a city, town, or place of business. For those that are not associated with a specific location, it is easiest to map it using GPS coordinates.

Luckily, Google has a system of codes that converts the coordinates into pin-drop locations that Google Maps can interpret and navigate.

Each adventure in this guide includes GPS coordinates along with a physical address whenever it is available.

It is important that you are prepared for poor cell signals. It is recommended that you route your location and ensure that the directions are accessible offline. Depending on your device and the distance of some locations, you may need to travel with a backup battery source.

About Maine

Maine is the northernmost state within the contiguous United States. Primarily known for its woodlands and mountains, it was also part of one of the first permanent European settlements in New England. The Popham Colony was established in 1607 by the Plymouth Company, which researchers believe was made up of the first European settlers in Maine.

Maine was admitted as a state on March 15, 1820, becoming the 23rd added to the Union. Originally part of Massachusetts, Maine was separated as a territory to enter the Union as a free state. After a heated debate divided the U.S. House of Representatives, this decision ultimately led to Maine's admittance to the United States as part of the Missouri Compromise.

Adopted in 1937, "State of Maine" is the state song. It was written and composed by Roger Vinton Snow, who died in 1953.

Today, there are still several Native American tribes living in parts of Maine, including the Penobscot Nation and the Passamaquoddy Tribe, residing in their ancestral homelands. According to the 2010 census, Maine has a population of 1,318,301.

Another well-known feature of Maine is its distinct dialect, referred to as Eastern New England English, which came from early explorers who landed on Maine's coast in the 16th century. The accent is most recognizable in the so-called "Down East" and "Mid Coast" regions.

Sightseeing is a popular activity in Maine, where visitors can enjoy many outdoor activities. Vacationers may choose to fish, hike, boat, or ski. There are also historical sites to explore like Old Orchard Beach. Maine has three national parks: Baxter State Park, Acadia National Park, and Isle Royale National Park. Other attractions include lighthouses such as the Marshall Point site located at the entrance to Port Clyde harbor.

Landscape and Climate

The Atlantic Ocean lies to the east of Maine. Forests cover more than half of the landmass, which is much less populated than other states in America. Coastal plains are located near the ocean, with hills rolling away toward the interior plateau. The foothills to the west gradually turn into mountains running north to south through the center of the state.

Glaciers formed rivers such as the Androscoggin, Kennebec, Penobscot, and St Croix during the last ice age. They carved steep gorges through mountain ranges, while coastal rivers flowed slowly over broad sandy plains. Maine's largest lake, Moosehead Lake, is located in the state's west-central region.

Maine's climate is transitional between the humid continental climate of New England and the milder Maritime Temperate Climate. Temperature averages range from 44°F in January to 68°F in July. Snowfall can vary from less than 10 inches along coastal areas to over 100 inches inland during winter months.

Spring, summer, and autumn are shorter seasons compared to the rest of the Northeast but are pleasant with ample rainfall throughout the year. Fog is common, especially along the Maine coastlines during the summer months when moist air comes from the Gulf of Maine. Strong winds blowing over the Atlantic Ocean during the winter produce sea-effect snowfall on Maine's Atlantic and inland areas.

Auburn Riverwalk

Located near the Great Falls of the Androscoggin River, the Auburn Riverwalk runs through the old mill district of the cities of Auburn and Lewiston. Lewiston is the second-largest city in Maine and offers some of the best dining in the state. In addition, Lewiston is home to the largest French-speaking population in the state.

The 1.6-mile-wide trail is excellent for beautiful scenery year round, and many residents and tourists make it part of their early-morning or nighttime routines. One section of the trail was built by the Grand Trunk Railroad in 1909. The Simard-Payne Memorial Park is toward one end where the river and trail join, featuring several benches and a paved loop to enjoy the beauty.

Best Time to Visit: You can visit any time of year, but winter snow can limit some activities such as biking.

Pass/Permit/Fees: Free

Closest City or Town: Auburn

Physical Address:
Simard-Payne Memorial Park
46 Beech Street
Lewiston, ME 04240

GPS Coordinates: 44.10522° N, 70.22535° W

Did You Know? The nearby Androscoggin River is known as the powerhouse that fueled the mill industry of the region.

Maine State House

The Maine State House is located in Augusta. In 1832, shortly after Maine became a state, plans for the capital began. The state hired famed architect Charles Bulfinch, who had previously designed the Massachusetts State House, portions of the U.S. Capitol, and several other civic buildings.

The beautiful Capital Park, a memorial, and a museum are nearby. The Cross Office building is toward the front entrance, featuring the Cross Café, which is famous for its dining.

Best Time to Visit: The Maine State House is open Monday through Friday from 8:00 a.m. to 5:00 p.m. Spring is the busiest season for tour groups.

Pass/Permit/Fees: Tours and entry are free.

Closest City or Town: Augusta

Physical Address:
Maine State House
Capitol Street and State Street
Augusta, ME 04330

GPS Coordinates: 44.68002° N, 69.83003° W

Did You Know? In 2014, the State House replaced its copper dome. Many of the scraps were used for souvenirs, and about 600 square feet was sold to artists for various projects.

The First Amendment Museum

The First Amendment Museum was built in 1911 by publishing tycoon William H. Gannett as a wedding gift for his son, who later founded Guy Gannett Publishing Company in 1921. Gannett and his publishing company were famous for their staunch support of the First Amendment, and they remained in business until 1998.

The museum is located just steps from the State Capitol building and the Governor's Mansion. After visiting the museum, pick up lunch from Wrapped Up, which features some of the best sandwiches in the area, and enjoy an outdoor meal at Capitol Park. Both spots are within a 5-minute walk from the museum.

Best Time to Visit: The museum is open Monday through Friday from 10 a.m. to 4 p.m.

Pass/Permit/Fees: Tours are free.

Closest City or Town: Augusta

Physical Address:
First Amendment Museum
184 State Street #6406
Augusta, ME 04330

GPS Coordinates: 44.30939° N, 69.78068° W

Did You Know? The museum holds the original "Bong Hits 4 Jesus" banner that led to the *Morse v. Frederick* Supreme Court case, which was critical in defining the limits of high school students' rights to free speech in 2007.

Bangor City Forest

The Rolland F. Perry City Forest spans an impressive 680 acres of wildlife habitat. It's also an actual "working forest" that's actively managed to generate revenue in Bangor.

The forest features more than 4 miles of access roads and almost 10 miles of other trails for jogging, biking, running, and cross-country skiing or horseshoeing in winter.

Owned and managed by the city of Bangor, the wildlife habitat is open year round and is home to several large animals such as deer, moose, bear, and Orono owls.

Best Time to Visit: The forest is open year round, but the summer months make up the peak camping season.

Pass/Permit/Fees: There is no fee to visit.

Closest City or Town: Bangor

Physical Address:
Bangor City Forest
54 Tripp Drive
Bangor, ME 04401

GPS Coordinates: 44.86386° N, 68.74045° W

Did You Know? The forest is a top destination for geocaching, an activity in which you look for hidden containers with a GPS device along with clues left by someone else, usually online. There are more than 30 caches to find throughout the forest.

Baxter State Park

This park is named after Percival P. Baxter, who made it his life's mission to protect Maine's wilderness. In 1930, Baxter purchased 6,000 acres of land—including Katahdin, Maine's highest peak—and donated it to the state on the condition that it stay undeveloped. Since then, various purchases and donations have grown the land to a total of over 200,000 acres, with 75 percent a designated wildlife sanctuary. The park has a year-round staff of 22, which balloons to roughly 60 people in the summer, including law enforcement, rangers, and administration. The park is home to a diverse wildlife population, including whitetail deer, moose, and black bears.

Best Time to Visit: Summer is peak visitor season. Visitors should use caution from December 1 through March 31 since rescue services are limited.

Pass/Permit/Fees: Visiting is free for in-state residents or in-state rental cars. All others must pay an entrance fee of $12.

Closest City or Town: Bangor

Physical Address:
Baxter State Park Headquarters
64 Balsam Drive
Millinocket, ME 04462

GPS Coordinates: 46.02795° N, 68.94286° W

Did You Know? The park is entirely self-funded through donor endowment, user fees, and donations, all of which are held in trust by Governor Baxter's Deeds of Trust.

Cascade Park

Cascade Park is a small half-mile area located just northeast of Maine Medical Center on State Street. Complete with a gazebo, walking trails, and large picnic tables, the park is a popular summer spot for picnics. Built in 1934, Cascade Park is known for several water features, including a 20-foot grotto and waterfall.

At night, the park's fountains are illuminated with many breathtaking multicolored lights. It is also a quick 10-minute walk from Coffee Express, where you can grab bakery snacks. Papa Gambino's Pizzas is nearby for a nice lunch in the park.

Best Time to Visit: May to September is the best time to visit.

Pass/Permit/Fees: Free

Closest City or Town: Bangor

Physical Address:
Cascade Park
600 State Street
Bangor, ME 04401

GPS Coordinates: 44.81183° N, 68.74591° W

Did You Know? While Bangor is a small, quiet town, it hasn't always been peaceful. In 1937, the bloodiest shootout in Maine's history occurred in Bangor between federal agents and Al Brady, a criminal gang leader who appeared on the FBI's Most Wanted list. There is a memorial on Central Street in memory of the agents lost.

Cole Land Transportation Museum

The Cole Land Transportation Museum hosts a marvelous collection of Maine land-transportation equipment, which is preserved by the Cole family. Its goal is to protect transportation history for future generations to enjoy.

The facility is highly focused on military heritage, as the Cole family has worked with the government on their equipment repair needs in every major war since World War I. The museum hopes to forever remind the public of the price people pay for freedom.

Best Time to Visit: The museum is open seasonally from May 1 to November 11 between the hours of 9 a.m. and 5 p.m.

Pass/Permit/Fees: Admission is $7 for adults, $5 for seniors ages 62 and up, $6 for AAA members, and free for children under the age of 19.

Closest City or Town: Bangor

Physical Address:
Cole Land Transportation Museum
405 Perry Road
Bangor, ME 04401

GPS Coordinates: 44.78601° N, 68.80481° W

Did You Know? The Cole family has run a truck and trailer business since 1917. Today, the company continues as A.J. Cole & Sons and employs over 100 mechanics.

Paul Bunyan Statue

American legend Paul Bunyan first appeared in advertisements in 1914 and later evolved through oral tradition into full-blown folklore. According to the tales, Paul Bunyan is a lumberjack accompanied by his trusty sidekicks, Babe the Blue Ox and Johnny Inkslinger. It is said he is a giant of a man who worked tirelessly through America's rough and wild conditions.

With the mythology claiming the folk hero's birthplace as Bangor, his 31-foot-high statue stands in Bass Park. The statue was given to the city by a group of builders from New York in 1959 for its 125th anniversary. There is an inscription claiming it is the largest Paul Bunyan statue in the world; however, that fact is debated.

Best Time to Visit: The statue is available year round, but the best weather is April through June.

Pass/Permit/Fees: Free

Closest City or Town: Bangor

Physical Address:
Paul Bunyan Statue
519 Main Street
Bangor, ME 04401

GPS Coordinates: 44.78932° N, 68.77837° W

Did You Know? The Paul Bunyan statue made an appearance in the Steven King film adaptation of *It*. However, a temporary statue was erected in the town of Port Hope, Ontario, where the sequel was filmed.

Stephen King's House

Famed horror author and Maine native Stephen King has published over 63 novels and 200 short stories. He uses the state as the setting for many of his books. King lived until recently in a unique mansion in downtown Bangor.

Although it is rumored that his house will eventually be transformed into a museum, it's currently not open to the public. However, the author's house is easily identifiable and able to be viewed from the sidewalk. The large red structure features a tower and is guarded by a wrought iron fence filled with spiders, winged creatures, and other creepy things.

Best Time to Visit: You can only drive by the property or look through the gates, so it's accessible any time of year.

Pass/Permit/Fees: Free

Closest City or Town: Bangor

Physical Address:
The Stephen & Tabitha King Foundation
47 W. Broadway
Bangor, ME 04401

GPS Coordinates: 44.80301° N, 68.78510° W

Did You Know? Stephen King moved out of the house in February 2021 after living there for many years.

Agamont Park

Located in Bar Harbor, Agamont Park was created on the site of an old house and hotel. With the original structure built in 1840 and transformed into a hotel before burning to the ground in 1888, Agamont has seen many seasons. As a favorite of tourists and locals alike, the park is settled on a hill offering 180-degree views of all the city's best features, including Frenchman Bay, its islands, and Mount Deseret narrows. The entrance is off Main Street and marked by a stunning water fountain designed by Eric Stodderholtz. Agamont Park's fountain has remained an iconic image for Bar Harbor since the 1930s and is often found on various media, including postcards.

Best Time to Visit: Summertime is a great time to visit since many of the beautiful flowers are in bloom. It is also a fantastic place to watch 4th of July fireworks.

Pass/Permit/Fees: Parking is available for $2 per hour.

Closest City or Town: Bar Harbor

Physical Address:
Agamont Park
One Main Street
Bar Harbor, ME 04609

GPS Coordinates: 44.39095° N, 68.20443° W

Did You Know? In October 2013, the television show *The O'Reilly Factor* sent one of its correspondents to Bar Harbor after the town council voted to remove the Wreaths Across America display that had been in the park since July 2011.

Cadillac Mountain

Cadillac Mountain is arguably the most significant destination for people visiting Acadia National Park. As the highest point on the East Coast, it offers a stunning view of the island landscape and glacier-spotted coast.

People love to trek up the mountain early in the morning to witness the beautiful sunrise. For those wishing to soak in the scenery from the comfort of their vehicle, the Cadillac Summit Road can be accessed via Park Loop Road and will bring visitors up to the 1,530-foot peak.

Best Time to Visit: Summer and fall are the busiest seasons, but early September has fewer crowds as well as spectacular weather and views.

Pass/Permit/Fees: Reservations are $6 per vehicle, and people can book a sunrise or daytime ticket. In addition, Acadia National Park passes are required, which are $30 per vehicle, $25 for motorcycles, and $15 for pedestrians. All passes are good for 7 days.

Closest City or Town: Bar Harbor

Physical Address:
Cadillac Mountain
Cadillac Summit Road
Bar Harbor, ME 04609

GPS Coordinates: 44.35294° N, 68.22512° W

Did You Know? It is known as the first place in the U.S. that you can see the sunrise, although that is only true for a portion of the year.

Carriage Roads

John D. Rockefeller Jr. built 45 miles of rustic carriage roads that weave around the scenic Acadia National Park. The roads were created to preserve the picturesque hillsides and save trees while also helping carriage travelers take advantage of the scenery. Today, hikers, joggers, bicyclists, and even horse-drawn carriages still share the paths to take in the beauty.

Best Time to Visit: Summer and fall are peak seasons, but early September has fewer crowds and good weather conditions.

Pass/Permit/Fees: Acadia National Park passes are required, which are $30 per vehicle, $25 for motorcycles, and $15 for pedestrians. All passes are good for 7 days. Tours cost $65 per person for 1 hour or $105 for 2 hours. Children ages 2 to 12 can receive a $10 discount, and infants under the age of 2 are free.

Closest City or Town: Bar Harbor

Physical Address:
Parkman Mountain Carriage Road Trailhead
Acadia National Park
Mt Desert, ME 04660

GPS Coordinates: 44.33466° N, 68.29307° W

Did You Know? The Acadia National Park carriage roads have been included in the National Register of Historic Places since 1994.

Champlain Mountain & Beehive Loop Trail

If you are looking for a rigorous hike ending with an amazing view, you need to add the Beehive Loop Trail to your list. This trail is one of four rung-and-ladder hikes found in Acadia National Park. Iron rungs protrude from the uneven rock faces to aid hikers. Although not the most physically exhausting trek, the trail includes a 450-foot cliff. The reward is a stunning view of Sand Beach, the Gulf of Maine, and Thunder Hole.

Best Time to Visit: The best time to visit is between March and October.

Pass/Permit/Fees: Acadia National Park passes are required at a cost of $30 for vehicles, $25 for motorcycles, and $15 for pedestrians. All passes are good for 7 days.

Closest City or Town: Bar Harbor

Physical Address:
Parking Lot
Park Loop Road
Bar Harbor, ME 04609

GPS Coordinates:
Beehive Trail: 44.33333° N, 68.18556° W
Champlain North Ridge Trail: 44.36551° N, 68.19387° W

Did You Know? Because of its steep ascent and switchbacks, Beehive Trail is known as one of the most-thrilling hikes in Acadia National Park, second only to Precipice Trail.

Frenchman Bay

Frenchman Bay is named after Samuel de Champlain, who arrived in the Gulf of Maine in September 1604. The Frenchman's goal was to find a place for the St. Croix French colony to resettle.

After chartering much of Maine's coast, Champlain went on to found Quebec, Canada, in 1608. The explorer is also known for launching expeditions through the Great Lakes, New York, and Ottawa River regions.

The bay is a large body of water between Mount Desert Island and Southern Maine. There are several small islands in the bay area to view, and some you can even visit. On your way there, be sure to enjoy a delicious breakfast of blueberry pancakes at Jordan's Restaurant.

Best Time to Visit: Between late spring and fall is the best time to visit. However, early September still has excellent views and weather but with fewer crowds.

Pass/Permit/Fees: Free

Closest City or Town: Bar Harbor

Physical Address: Frenchman Bay is located off the coast of Bar Harbor, ME 04609.

GPS Coordinates: 44.43487° N, 68.22244° W

Did You Know? Frenchman Bay is considered "Down East" by locals, which is the eastern coastal region of the counties Washington and Hancock.

Thunder Hole

Thunder Hole is a small inlet in Acadia National Park. If the timing is right, with the wind blowing and the ocean rising at half-tide, waves are forced into a granite crevice, causing the water to explode upward. The forced expulsion of air and water sounds like thunder.

Even if the waves happen to be calm during your visit, as most likely they will be, Thunder Hole is still a great place to stand on the rocks and enjoy the mountain and ocean views of Mount Desert Island.

Best Time to Visit: Between late spring and fall is the best time to visit. However, early September still has lovely views and weather but with fewer crowds.

Pass/Permit/Fees: Acadia National Park passes are required at a cost of $30 for vehicles, $25 for motorcycles, and $15 for pedestrians. All passes are good for 7 days.

Closest City or Town: Bar Harbor

Physical Address:
Thunder Hole
Park Loop Road
Bar Harbor, ME 04609

GPS Coordinates: 44.32092° N, 68.18833° W

Did You Know? Rogue waves can and do happen. In 2009, when Hurricane Bill was over 300 miles out to sea, a rogue wave swept three people into the open ocean. Use caution when visiting during adverse weather and keep children close.

Swan's Island

Swan's Island lies 6 miles southwest of Mount Desert Island and Acadia National Park. The town dates back to 1897, but its history starts long before then. Colonel James Swan established the Swan's Island plantation in 1765. Prior to that, a colonial settlement existed on the island until it was attacked in 1750 by the indigenous population The settlement dissolved when the Whidden family was taken hostage and sold into the Canadian slave trade.

Today, the remote island has regular ferry service to and from the mainland. Some of the island attractions include historic homes dating to the 1700s, a lighthouse, a beautiful beach, hiking trails, and a lobster and marine museum.

Best Time to Visit: Swan Island is open seasonally from mid-May to October.

Pass/Permit/Fees: Ferry fees are $12.50 for adults, $6.25 for minors, and $31 for a vehicle with a driver.

Closest City or Town: Bass Harbor

Physical Address:
Maine State Ferry Services
114 Granville Road
Bass Harbor, ME 04653

GPS Coordinates: 44.18697° N, 68.42247° W

Did You Know? In early August, Swan's Island hosts a three-night music festival on the water. Beautiful sailboats and other craft take to the waves for their musical performances.

Belfast City Park

Founded in 1904, Belfast City Park spans 17.5 acres overlooking Penobscot Bay. Recognized as the oldest park in the area, it is a favorite of tourists and locals alike during the spring, summer, and fall months. Visitors can enjoy tennis courts, a barbeque space, a swimming pool, a ballpark, gardens, and even a children's theme park.

Throughout Belfast, visitors will find information boards accounting for the history of the area. These are all a part of a city project called *The Museum in the Streets*. Belfast City Park hosts one of these markers, and there are eight others within a mile's walk.

Best Time to Visit: The park is open May through November. However, it closes daily from 11:00 p.m. until 6:00 a.m.

Pass/Permit/Fees: There is no fee to visit.

Closest City or Town: Belfast

Physical Address:
Belfast City Park
City Park Road
Belfast, ME 04915

GPS Coordinates: 44.41552° N, 68.99313° W

Did You Know? Belfast City Park was founded by the Belfast Improvement Society, a group of local women activists who set out to improve residents' experience in education, arts, and recreation.

Grafton Notch State Park

Stretching over 3,129 acres, Grafton Notch State Park is in the Mahoosuc Range, nestled between Old Speck Mountain and Baldpate Mountain. Although most of the trails in this park are difficult, including a 12-mile stretch along the Appalachian Trail, there are a few for the less-experienced hiker as well.

The trek to Screw Auger Falls is considered easy. The trail to the 23-foot waterfall usually takes adventurers less than 5 minutes to complete. The Bear River feeds the falls, and the area is a local favorite for families to enjoy a swim and a pleasant lunch. For those who are less adept at hiking, hunting and fishing are available. During the winter, visitors can enjoy cross-country skiing and snowmobiling.

Best Time to Visit: Mid-May to mid-October is best.

Pass/Permit/Fees: Admission is $3 for Maine residents and $4 for nonresidents.

Closest City or Town: Oxford

Physical Address:
Grafton Notch State Park
Bear River Road
Newry, ME 04261

GPS Coordinates: 44.61675° N, 70.90654° W

Did You Know? On the Maine Birding Trail, you can see eagles, falcons, and migratory songbirds. Larger animals like bears and moose may also appear.

Maine Mineral & Gem Museum

In 1972, one of the largest chunks of tourmaline was unearthed in Western Maine, spurring a geological legacy within the state. The Maine Mineral and Gem Museum features some of the largest collections of gems, minerals, and extraterrestrial materials within its exhibits. Beyond the vast array of stones, the museum works to cultivate an educational environment showcasing a detailed geological history of Maine. This museum also holds a lunar and asteroid-belt meteorite collection designed to increase knowledge of the solar system. It's home to one of the largest chunks of moon rocks in the world. Visitors will also find many interactive exhibits of minerals and gems.

Best Time to Visit: The museum is open Monday through Saturday from 10 a.m. to 5 p.m. and 11 a.m. to 5 p.m. on Sunday. It's closed on Tuesday.

Pass/Permit/Fees: Admission is $15 for adults, $12 for seniors, and $10 for students. Children ages 12 and under are free.

Closest City or Town: Bethel

Physical Address:
Maine Mineral and Gem Museum
99 Main Street
Bethel, ME 04217

GPS Coordinates: 44.40837° N, 70.78866° W

Did You Know? The Maine Mineral & Gem Museum contains the largest piece of the planet Mars known to be located on Earth.

Rangeley Lake State Park

Rangeley State Park is located in the western mountains of Maine. The 870-acre recreational site was created in 1960 and cost the state $595,000. This area offers hiking, camping, hunting, and many more activities for visitors. The 9-mile-wide lake is filled with salmon and trout for catch-and-release fishing. Although there are multiple trails, the South Bog Trail is one of the most popular. This moderate hike is just under 5 miles and usually takes visitors around 2 hours to finish. It is advised to map out the trail prior to hiking as portions of it are not well marked. Mushroom hunters will have the most luck in early October, and dogs are welcome as long as they are properly leashed.

Best Time to Visit: The best time of year to visit is from May 1 to October 1. The park is open 9 a.m. to sunset.

Pass/Permit/Fees: For Maine residents, admission is $4 for adults and free for children under the age of 5 or seniors ages 65 and up. For nonresidents, admission is $6 for adults, $2 for seniors, and $1 for children ages 5 to 11.

Closest City or Town: Bethel

Physical Address:
Rangeley Lake State Park
1 State Park Road
Rangeley, ME 04970

GPS Coordinates: 45.00265° N, 70.70873° W

Did You Know? A sign in town says that Rangeley is the halfway point between the equator and the north pole!

The Sunday River Bridge

The Sunday River Bridge, also known as the Artist's Bridge, is one of Maine's most-famous covered bridges. Built in 1872, the 100-foot covered structure is known for being a favorite among photographers and painters. The iconic wooden bridge spans over the stunning Sunday River, framed by the lush green foliage of Maine's forests. At one point in time, the Sunday River Bridge was a main thoroughfare until the road was re-routed in 1955. Despite this bridge being an iconic Maine image since the Civil War, it is not the original structure. The bridge has been re-built many times since its initial construction in 1811. Due to the Sunday River's seasonal flooding, the bridge was washed out in 1869, again in 1871, and a third time in 1927. It has remained closed to traffic since 1958, but visitors can still marvel at its beauty from the same vantage points as artists have over the centuries.

Best Time to Visit: Any time of year is great to visit.

Pass/Permit/Fees: Free

Closest City or Town: Bethel

Physical Address:
Sunday River Bridge
Sunday River Road
Newry, ME 04261

GPS Coordinates: 44.49300° N, 70.84329° W

Did You Know? It is said that the first artist to capture this bridge's beauty was Civil War POW and Union soldier John Enneking.

Fortunes Rocks Beach

Fortunes Rocks Beach is named after an American privateer who shipwrecked and washed up onto the shore in the late 1700s. Francis Fortune found farm work with the Rossiter couple who lived nearby. When the owner of the farm died, Francis married his widow, Peggy, and the couple built a legacy in the area. The couple's graves are marked by large marble slabs and are now known as Fortunes Rocks. The 2 miles of hard-packed beach stretch from Biddeford Pool to Fortunes Rocks, making the area a great spot for visitors to relax and swim. The sand is firm enough for walking and jogging. In addition, people also come for surfing, bodyboarding, and other fun wave activities. It's important to know that Fortunes Rocks Beach does not offer any facilities.

Best Time to Visit: Visit from May to September when lifeguards are on duty.

Pass/Permit/Fees: Limited parking is available for $22 per day by permit only.

Closest City or Town: Biddeford

Physical Address:
Fortunes Rocks Beach
Fortunes Rocks Road
Biddeford, ME 04005

GPS Coordinates: 43.43314° N, 70.37170° W

Did You Know? Fortunes Rocks Beach is a popular place for visitors to hunt for and find sea glass!

Old Canada Road Scenic Byway

The Old Canada Road is 78 miles long and travels from Solon to the Canadian border. Travelers can enjoy the views of nature along the ride in addition to stopping at several villages along the way for eating and exploring. The road offers scenery of the Kennebec River, Wyman Lake, mountains, and forests. There are rest stops that serve as both scenic points and waystations.

Originally, the byway was a logging route with sparse populations along the road. There were only a few villages settled in the area. From 1820 to 1860, the byway was the main route between Maine and Canada, which led to a large flux of French-Canadian immigrants into the area.

Best Time to Visit: The ideal time to see the foliage is in the fall from late September to early October.

Pass/Permit/Fees: Free

Closest City or Town: Bingham

Physical Address:
Old Canada Road Scenic Byway
356 Main Street
Bingham, ME 04920

GPS Coordinates: 45.06336° N, 69.88168° W

Did You Know? The Old Canada Road used to be a route for trade and even a path for immigrants from Quebec to the Atlantic.

Coastal Maine Botanical Gardens

The Coastal Maine Botanical Gardens spreads across 300 acres and is home to the famous *Guardians of the Seeds* art installment created by Thomas Dambo. Throughout the Maine woodlands, massive sculptures of trolls emerge from the landscape, inciting travelers to ground themselves in nature. Although these legendary creations have become the most visible on social media, visitors can experience several exhibits and explore different flower gardens, lawns, and ponds as well. There is a special garden for children in addition to a native-bee exhibit and a native-butterfly and moth house.

Best Time to Visit: This attraction is open May through October from 9 a.m. to 5 p.m.

Pass/Permit/Fees: Admission is $22 for adults, $18 for seniors and veterans, $15 for students over the age of 18, and $10 for children ages 3 to 7. Children under the age of 3 and members are free.

Closest City or Town: Boothbay

Physical Address:
Coastal Maine Botanical Gardens
132 Botanical Gardens Drive
Boothbay, ME 04537

GPS Coordinates: 43.87275° N, 69.65891° W

Did You Know? For a week in August, visitors can see the Caterpillar Lab to learn about all different types of caterpillars and how they are cared for at the gardens.

Hog Island

Before Hog Island was purchased by colonizing settlers in the 1600s, it was home to the Wawenock tribe of the Abenaki-Penobscot group. *Wawenock* translates to "round island." The English paid for the deaths of the Penobscot, but most of the Indigenous people of Hog Island died from smallpox and other European illnesses. Today, the 300-acre island is famous for its Audubon Camp, which specializes in the preservation of the Atlantic puffin and the black-capped chickadee. The island's modern name was derived from the wild hogs roaming free when European settlers colonized the area. In 1908, Dr. David Todd and Mabel Loomis Todd transformed the island into a conservation haven. Starting at the visitor center, take the Hockomock Point Trail, an easy 1-mile hike winding through red oak and spruce trees.

Best Time to Visit: Visit from May through September.

Pass/Permit/Fees: Individually priced packages are available for ferry services and Audubon Camp packages.

Closest City or Town: Bremen

Physical Address:
Hog Island Audubon Camp
12 Audubon Road
Bremen, ME 04551

GPS Coordinates: 43.98888° N, 69.42070° W

Did You Know The Audubon Camp is a favorite for naturalists and even lured the inventor of the field guide, Roger Tory Peterson, to teach at the camp in 1936.

Chamberlain Freedom Park

Chamberlain Freedom Park is the only official memorial for the Underground Railroad in the state of Maine. Although Maine was a less common route than New Hampshire, most runaway slaves attempted to escape from the United States to Canada by trekking through Evan's Notch. In 1995, one of the oldest homes in Brewer, the Holyoke House, revealed a secret tunnel during its deconstruction. It was discovered that both the home and tunnel were one of the few routes used by runaway slaves during the 19th century. In 2002, the *North to Freedom* statue was installed, which features a slave emerging from the entrance. The park itself is named after Brigadier General Joshua Chamberlain, a Medal of Honor recipient recognized for his service in the Union Army during the Battle of Gettysburg.

Best Time to Visit: This park is nice to visit year-round.

Pass/Permit/Fees: Free

Closest City or Town: Brewer

Physical Address:
Chamberlain Freedom Park
State Street
Brewer, ME 04412

GPS Coordinates: 44.79934° N, 68.76229° W

Did You Know? The memorial was partially funded through a contribution from Stephen and Tabitha King.

Katahdin Iron Works

The Katahdin Iron Works was the only 19th-century operation of its kind in Maine. The iron works operated from 1845 to 1890 and now exists as a historical site. All that remains of the old infrastructure are a single furnace and charcoal kiln. Although the Katahdin Iron Works was not the most successful due to outside competition, it did lead to the creation of a town, roads, and even a private portion of the railroad. Visitors to the old ironworks can also see Gulf Hagas canyon near the west branch of Pleasant River. Ironically, during the heyday of the Katahdin Iron Works, the forests in this area were greatly depleted. Today, Gulf Hagas is dubbed the "Grand Canyon of the East" and cuts through 100 miles of rich forests surrounding Maine's portion of the Appalachian Trail. This area is also home to a grove of eastern white pine known as the Hermitage.

Best Time to Visit: Summer is the ideal season to visit.

Pass/Permit/Fees: Admission is $10 per person or $6 for Maine residents.

Closest City or Town: Brownville

Physical Address:
Katahdin Iron Works State Historic Site
Ki Road
Brownville, ME 04414

GPS Coordinates: 45.44618° N, 69.17454° W

Did You Know? The name *Katahdin* means "Greatest Mountain." It was chosen by the Penobscot Indians.

Maine Maritime Museum

Established in 1962, the Maine Maritime Museum spans over 20 acres along the Kennebec River and is home to one of America's only wooden shipyards. In addition to exhibits accounting for the rich history along the river, the museum is also home to a 1906 schooner and functional boat shop. Known as "The City of Ships," Bath began shipbuilding in the 1600s, starting with small, family-made boats. It continued to develop its craft on a larger scale through the 17th and 18th centuries. Eventually, Bath Iron Works was founded, which became famous for building much of the U.S. Navy's fleet. At the museum, visitors can learn about the area's rich history, walk through the shipyards, enjoy immersive exhibits, visit preserved Victorian homes and shops, and learn about the day-to-day lives of local shipbuilding families.

Best Time to Visit: Summer is the busiest time, but there are smaller crowds and Christmas lights in the winter.

Pass/Permit/Fees: Admission is $18 for adults, $16.50 for seniors, and free for guests under the age of 18.

Closest City or Town: Bath

Physical Address:
Maine Maritime Museum
243 Washington Street
Bath, ME 04530

GPS Coordinates: 43.89469° N, 69.81609° W

Did You Know? The kids' area includes a pirate ship, a human-sized lobster trap, and more!

Peary-MacMillan Arctic Museum

Named for Robert E. Peary and Donald B. MacMillan, 19th-century explorers and graduates of Bowdoin, the Peary-MacMillan Arctic Museum offers educational exhibits about Arctic exploration. In addition, this museum continues to support research and study of the Arctic environment and its cultures.

Both Peary and MacMillan donated collections of equipment, notes, specimen, and photos of their Arctic exploration and expeditions. Exhibits also feature art and models of transportation devices such as kayaks.

Best Time to Visit: The Peary-MacMillan Arctic Museum is an excellent place to visit any time. Be sure to check the website for visiting information, as reservations are now required.

Pass/Permit/Fees: There is no fee to visit.

Closest City or Town: Brunswick

Physical Address:
Peary-MacMillan Arctic Museum
9 Campus Road S
Brunswick, ME 04011

GPS Coordinates: 43.90806° N, 69.96292° W

Did You Know? The museum sells Peary and Henson dolls, encouraging visitors to take them along on adventures worldwide and send photos to the museum.

Popham Beach State Park

Popham Beach State Park is near Fox and Wood islands as well as the Kennebec and Morse rivers. Established in 1607, Popham Colony only survived a year before being abandoned in 1608. Despite its short history, the colony is famous for building the first ship in North America.

Visitors enjoy swimming, surfing, and collecting shells along the beach. Though lifeguards are present in the summer, it's important to know that this beach features a strong surf and undertows. Dogs are welcome at Popham Beach State Park from October 1 through March 31 as long as they are kept on a leash. No pets are allowed the rest of the year.

Best Time to Visit: Although the park is open all year from 9 a.m. to sunset, it is best to visit during the summer when lifeguards are present.

Pass/Permit/Fees: Admission is $6 for residents and $8 for nonresidents.

Closest City or Town: Bath

Physical Address:
Popham Beach State Park
711 Popham Road
Phippsburg, ME 04562

GPS Coordinates: 43.73885° N, 69.79777° W

Did You Know? Horses are allowed on this beach from October 1 through March 31 as long as you have a beach permit for your horse.

Reid State Park

In 1946, Walter E. Reid donated the 770 acres of land that now make up Reid State Park, which became the first saltwater beach owned by Maine. The park is one of the few places in the state where visitors can find sand beaches and dunes. It is also well-known for its lagoons, salt marshes, and tidepools. Although it is always wise to exercise caution near the ocean, this is a prime location for open-water swimming and tidal exploration.

The Mile Beach Walk is an easy hike that usually takes around 35 minutes for visitors to complete. Although this hike between Maine's coasts and forests is beautiful, it is also popular and tends to attract insects. Many people spot eider ducks, piping plovers, terns, and seals.

Best Time to Visit: Any time is great to visit.

Pass/Permit/Fees: Admission is $6 for residents or $8 for nonresidents.

Closest City or Town: Bath

Physical Address:
Reid State Park
375 Seguinland Road
Georgetown, ME 04548

GPS Coordinates: 43.77957° N, 69.72783° W

Did You Know? There is also a smaller park atop Griffith Head that allows views of the lighthouses on Seguin Island, Hendricks Head, and The Cuckolds.

Coos Canyon

Off State Highway 17, visitors can enjoy the rampaging torrents of the Swift River as they cut through Coos Canyon. Coos Canyon is known for its waterfalls, picturesque picnics, cliff jumping, swimming hole, camping, and promise of riches! In 1886, a gazetteer (a geographical index) identified Coos Canyon as a hotspot for gold and other minerals. As legend goes, the Swift River carries the precious gold flakes from a mother lode upstream. Coos Canyon is also known for its unique rock formation, which features smooth curves and gives the water a signature shade of green. The metamorphic rock is estimated to date back over 400 million years, and the canyon cuts through what is known as the Silurian Perry Mountain Formation.

Best Time to Visit: Between April and November is the idea time to visit when the spring thaws and rains increase the depth and flow of the river.

Pass/Permit/Fees: There is no fee to visit.

Closest City or Town: Byron

Physical Address:
Coos Canyon Rest Area
472 ME-17
Byron, ME 04275

GPS Coordinates: 44.72337° N, 70.63201° W

Did You Know? The rocks that make up the canyon walls feature what look like carved lines that have been caused by erosion across time.

Height of Land

Height of Land is a scenic viewpoint along the Rangeley Lakes Scenic Byway. This spot offers views of the Rangeley Lakes region surrounded by the mountains of western Maine. The area stretches over 512 acres. As one of the most famous lookouts in Maine, this destination is a must-see point during the fall. The sweeping views from Height of Land lets visitors fully take in New England's breathtaking, diverse autumn scene of green, red, yellow, and orange leaves.

Initially, this viewpoint was a "pull-off" by the side of the road, which posed a danger due to oncoming traffic. Currently, Height of Land has an expanded parking and viewing area, enhancing everyone's safety and enjoyment.

Best Time to Visit: Autumn offers the best views for beautiful foliage colors.

Pass/Permit/Fees: There is no fee to visit.

Closest City or Town: Byron

Physical Address:
Height of Land
ME-17
Roxbury, ME 04275

GPS Coordinates: 44.84123° N, 70.71013° W

Did You Know? This viewpoint is considered one of the most picturesque places not just in Maine but in New England overall.

Bartlettyarns Mill

Bartlettyarns Mill has a history beginning in 1821 when Ozias Bartlett started a carding mill. That was in operation on the banks of Higgins Stream until the 1920s when the original building burned down. However, a new building was created that offered the convenience of electricity. This spinning mule is in daily operation and is the only remaining one of its kind in the U.S. The machinery spins 240 bobbins to replicate hand spinning for fine yarn that is known for its softness and airiness.

Visitors can tour the mill during their annual open house. Although it's wise to check their website for changes, the open house usually hosts tours on August 2 and 3 from 10:00 a.m. to 4:00 p.m.

Best Time to Visit: Bartlettyarn Mill's store is open Monday through Friday from 8:30 a.m. to 4:30 p.m. except on holidays. To take a full tour, visit during the mill's open house in August.

Pass/Permit/Fees: There is no fee to visit.

Closest City or Town: Cambridge

Physical Address:
Bartlettyarns, Inc.
20 Water Street
Harmony, ME 04942

GPS Coordinates: 44.97184° N, 69.54680° W

Did You Know? Bartlettyarns Mill was featured in the film adaptation of Stephen King's *Graveyard Shift*.

Bald Mountain Preserve

Bald Mountain Preserve receives its name from its summit, which is bare rock, or "bald," in terms of vegetation. The preserve encompasses 583 acres and is maintained by the Coastal Mountains Land Trust. The peak reaches 1,280 feet and is home to a unique habitat of alpine plants.

There is a 2.6-mile trail round trip for visitors to explore the forest leading up to the summit, which is made up of exposed ledges. At the peak, there are beautiful views of western Penobscot Bay and other coastal mountains. There is no camping allowed, and fires are prohibited. In addition, visitors should not remove any of the native vegetation.

Best Time to Visit: Visitors are welcome year round, though the trail may become icy in the winter.

Pass/Permit/Fees: Resident admission is $4 for adults and free for children under the age of 5 or seniors over the age of 64. Nonresident admission is $6 for adults, $2 for seniors, and $1 for children ages 5 to 11.

Closest City or Town: Camden

Physical Address:
Bald Mountain Preserve
325 Barnestown Road
Camden, ME 04843

GPS Coordinates: 44.23390° N, 69.14153° W

Did You Know? The mountain is home to smooth sandwort, which is indigenous only to this region and has been reported in only 25 area towns.

Camden Harbor Park and Amphitheatre

Camden Harbor Park and Amphitheatre are actually two parks that opened in 1931 as gifts of a local philanthropist named Mary Louise Curtis Bok Zimbalist. Zimbalist wanted the parks to enhance the appearance of the renovated Camden Library.

The parks were completely restored in the early 2000s as a community project funded by taxpayers and donors. Restorations included repaving paths, planting trees and flowers, replacing benches, and adding a wheelchair-accessible entrance.

Best Time to Visit: Spring through fall is the best time to visit.

Pass/Permit/Fees: There is no fee to visit.

Closest City or Town: Camden

Physical Address:
Harbor Park
120-1968
Camden, ME 04843

GPS Coordinates: 44.21392° N, 69.06397° W

Did You Know? Zimbalist chose the Olmsted brothers, who were famous architects, to design the parks.

Camden Hills State Park

Established in the 1930s, Camden Hills State Park is made up of over 5,000 acres overlooking Penobscot Bay. Visitors can view this bay as well as Camden Harbor from Mount Battie by driving up to the 800-foot summit. In addition to the views, visitors can hike a 25-mile trail system that started as a carriage road in 1897. Atop the summit, there is a stone tower that stands in the same spot Columbus Bushwell originally built the Summit House, which was torn down in 1920. It wasn't until 1948 that Mount Battie joined Camden Hills State Park. Now visitors can hike an easy 1.2-mile trail or explore the old carriage roads from the past. Camping is permitted year round, and Camden Hills offers various recreational facilities for visitors.

Best Time to Visit: Visit from May to November, as winter and spring may result in closures depending on the weather conditions.

Pass/Permit/Fees: Admission is $4 for residents or $6 for nonresidents.

Closest City or Town: Camden

Physical Address:
Camden Hills State Park
280 Belfast Road
Camden, Maine 04843

GPS Coordinates: 44.23151° N, 69.04813° W

Did You Know? This park inspired the poem "Renascence" by Edna St. Vincent Millay.

Curtis Island Lighthouse

Curtis Island Lighthouse was built in 1835 but moved to Curtis Island in 1896 to stand at the entrance to Camden Harbor. It is a registered historical site, though the lighthouse is considered private property. Surrounding the lighthouse is a public park, which can be accessed by visitors via sightseeing boats in Camden Harbor. Visitors can also view the lighthouse from the area of Curtis Island Overlook. The lighthouse and island received its current name in 1934 after the publisher of the *Saturday Evening Post*, Cyrus H.K. Curtis. Curtis summered in Camden and even donated the facilities that are now used by the Camden Yacht Club.

Best Time to Visit: Spring and summer are the best seasons to visit since boat access is limited in colder months.

Pass/Permit/Fees: The actual lighthouse is not accessible to the public, but the park is free. There is a fee for access to the island via boat.

Closest City or Town: Camden

Physical Address:
Curtis Lighthouse Overlook
148 Bay View Street
Camden, ME 04843

GPS Coordinates: 44.20002° N, 69.05575° W

Did You Know? According to a 1922 article, Curtis Island was originally named after a Black cook who admired the island when sailing past it in 1769.

High Street Historic District

High Street Historic District has been preserved to look as it did in the 19th century and has remained nearly unchanged since the 1920s. Starting at the crosshairs of Atlantic and Maine, the buildings along High Street showcase 19th and early 20th-century architecture. Visitors can see the public library, early 1800s farmhouses, and Harbor Park.

One of the most famous estates on High Street is the Queen Anne–style Norumbega Castle and Carriage House, designed by Arthur B. Jennings and built in 1886 by Joseph Barker Stearns. The castle is now an inn hosting guests for overnight stays and events.

Best Time to Visit: Any time of year is great to visit.

Pass/Permit/Fees: There is no fee to visit.

Closest City or Town: Camden

Physical Address:
High Street Historic District
High Street
Camden, ME 04843

GPS Coordinates: 44.21776° N, 69.05801° W

Did You Know? Dating back to 1633, High Street is one of the oldest continuously operating streets in the United States.

Wild Blueberry Land

Wild Blueberry Land is a family-owned farm that was built in 2001. Visitors will enjoy the theme of this Maine fruit throughout the landscape and museum. This educational farm presents the history of the wild blueberry in addition to sustainable farming methods and the health benefits of this fruit.

To remember this family-friendly place, visitors can purchase homemade pies, breads, jellies, and other delicious blueberry goods from the on-site bakery and gift shop.

Best Time to Visit: Wild Blueberry Land is only open during the summer and fall. From June 24 through September 7, it is open all week from 9:00 a.m. to 2:00 p.m. From September 8 through October 11, it is open Friday through Monday from 9:00 a.m. to 2:00 p.m. Every year, Wild Blueberry Land closes for Indigenous People's Day.

Pass/Permit/Fees: There is no fee to visit.

Closest City or Town: Columbia Falls

Physical Address:
Wild Blueberry Land
1067 US-1
Columbia Falls, ME 04623

GPS Coordinates: 44.64918° N, 67.70699° W

Did You Know? Wild Blueberry Land is believed to be home to the world's largest artificial blueberry!

Kefauver Studio Gallery

Will Kefauver is the signature member of the National Society of Artists and former vice president of the Kent Art Association. As a Maine local, his studio gallery in Damariscotta showcases his new works with various shows throughout the season. Kefauver is known for the lifelike intensity of his oil paintings. His subjects include the Monhegan and Pemaquid lighthouses, portraits of people and animals, and various mountain and forest scenes from around Maine. Previous seasons at the gallery showcased Kefauver's perspective of the waves and rocky coast. Visitors can buy Kefauver's works, and the gallery hosts art classes for beginners and skilled artists. Classes feature open-air lessons on how to paint the Maine landscape. Programs last 5–10 weeks, but walk-ins are welcome to join any class if seats are available.

Best Time to Visit: The gallery is open from June through January.

Pass/Permit/Fees: It's free to visit the gallery, but the price per painting will vary.

Closest City or Town: Damariscotta

Physical Address:
Kefauver Studio & Gallery
144 Bristol Road
Damariscotta, ME 04543

GPS Coordinates: 44.02277° N, 69.52697° W

Did You Know? Two more Kefauver studio galleries are located in Portland and New Harbor.

Thompson Ice House

Thompson Ice House is the only active ice-harvesting facility in Maine and one of the few still active in the country. For nearly 200 years, the Thompson family supplied ice to the families and merchants of Maine—most importantly the fishmongers shipping shellfish across the country. The Thompson Ice House remained in operation until 1985. Today, as a nonprofit museum, it hosts the annual Ice Harvest every February. The event is for local and visiting families who want to put their ice-harvesting skills to the test. Everyone will have an opportunity to saw through the ice and enjoy a warm cup of hot cocoa or coffee after. The museum features ice-harvesting tools, video presentations, and exhibits on other historic Maine traditions. In addition, a new building was erected in 2022 to showcase more historical exhibits.

Best Time to Visit: The museum is open from July to August, but visit in February to catch the annual Ice Harvest.

Pass/Permit/Fees: It's free to visit.

Closest City or Town: Damariscotta

Physical Address:
Thompson Ice House
4568 ME-129
South Bristol, ME 04568

GPS Coordinates: 43.878889° N, 69.560556° W

Did You Know? The harvested ice is used to make ice cream at the Annual Ice Cream Social in July.

Whaleback Shell Midden State Historic Site

Middens tell the story of prehistoric Maine's native peoples and coastal climate. Archeologists carbon date the ceramic pots and stone tools found in Whaleback Shell Midden to between 1,000 to 2,000 years old. Before it was designated a historic site, the midden stretched back nearly 400 feet away from the river. However, it was slowly depleted by looters and shell and fertilizer companies that ground the ancient oysters into chicken feed. You can hike a half-mile trail to see what remains of the Whaleback Shell Midden. The trailhead leads through an apple orchard and loops along the east side of the Damariscotta River. It features two scenic overlooks: one at the entrance of the orchard and the other on the bank of the river. Visitors are welcome to explore the 11-acre site year round.

Best Time to Visit: Visit between July and August for the best view.

Pass/Permit/Fees: It's free to hike and visit the site.

Closest City or Town: Damariscotta

Physical Address:
Whaleback Shell Midden State Historic Site
535 Main Street
Damariscotta, ME 04543

GPS Coordinates: 44.04230° N, 69.51197° W

Did You Know? Originally, the Whaleback Shell Midden was up to 15 feet deep.

Barred Island Preserve

Wear comfortable shoes when hiking in Barred Island Preserve. The 2.5-mile out-and-back trail is wet if you miss low tide, and much of the path is overrun with roots and moss. However, the trail leads to the quiet beach of Barred Island, which is perfect for swimming in the summer months. Barred Island Preserve is a nature sanctuary, and visitors can catch signs of wildlife on the trail. The hike is ideal for birdwatchers—you'll spy thrushes, blue-headed vireos, and more. The final quarter mile of the trail leads to a glaciated cliff's edge where you might catch sight of yellowthroats and song sparrows. The parking lot is located on Goose Cove Road but can fill up quickly. It's recommended that visitors come back later if the lot is packed as the trail is situated between two privately owned forests.

Best Time to Visit: Hike the trail at low tide between August and October.

Pass/Permit/Fees: It's free to visit and hike Barred Island Preserve.

Closest City or Town: Deer Isle

Physical Address:
Barred Island Preserve Parking
Goose Cove Road
Deer Isle, ME 04627

GPS Coordinates: 44.174136° N, 68.713753° W

Did You Know? The sandbar to Barred Island is only accessible twice a day during low tide.

Cobscook Bay State Park

Cobscook is a Malecite–Passamaquoddy word that means "boiling tide," which is precisely what happens at Cobscook Bay State Park twice a day. These powerful tides, combined with the prehistoric glacial activity, inspired the distinct geology visitors can explore in the park. The unique estuary ecosystem of Cobscook Bay makes it one of the most evocative places to fish, birdwatch, and otherwise spy on wildlife in Maine. Otters, seals, and over 200 species of bird, including the bald eagle, make their home in Cobscook Bay State Park. Families are invited to camp, fish, boat, and hike in the area. The Nature Trail (1.2 miles) and Shore Trail (0.75 miles) are both easy hikes that lead to campsites. Nature Trail features a lookout over Whiting Bay and Burnt Cove.

Best Time to Visit: The park is open year round, but the best time to camp is between August and October.

Pass/Permit/Fees: Camping fees are $6 per person or $20 per family for residents. Nonresident fees are $12 per person or $30 per family.

Closest City or Town: Dennysville

Physical Address:
Cobscook Bay State Park
40 S. Edmunds Road
Dennysville, Me 04628

GPS Coordinates: 44.84066° N, 67.15082° W

Did You Know? During high tide, the water can rise 24 feet.

L.C. Bates Museum

The L.C. Bates Museum houses unique curiosities from the 19th century. George Walter Hinkley, the founder of the collection, started accumulating donations of rocks and fossils in the 1890s. At that time, the museum was a school for boys, and the stalactites, sulfur rocks, and fossils he collected were used in the curriculum. Today, guests can peruse over 10,000 artifacts, including animal skeletons and wooly mammoth teeth. Hinkley valued the importance of an education and incorporated Maine's natural landscape into his lessons. Nature trails surround the museum, and students have erected monuments along the paths over the years. Dartmouth Trail starts near the museum entrance, but the Sunset Trailhead is by the bird sanctuary on Green Road. Visitors are also encouraged to visit the bird sanctuary, observatory, and butterfly garden during spring.

Best Time to Visit: Visit between April and November.

Pass/Permit/Fees: Admission is $3 for adults and $1 for children under the age of 18.

Closest City or Town: Fairfield

Physical Address:
L.C. Bates Museum
14 Easler Road
Hinckley, ME 04944

GPS Coordinates: 44.6625° N, 69.627778° W

Did You Know? Most of the museum displays were built in the 1920s and have been preserved to maintain the museum's turn-of-the-century quality.

Smalls Falls

Smalls Falls is a collection of four different waterfalls set in a colorful gorge. The half-mile trail to the first waterfall is easy, and you will cross a footbridge to continue up to the remaining three falls. The maximum elevation of this trail is 32 feet. The first waterfall is only 3 feet tall, but it cascades into a deep, 20-foot pool that guests can swim in during the summer. Further up are a 14-foot horsetail and a 25-foot segmented waterfall, followed by the final 12-foot slide waterfall. Overall, Smalls Falls reaches a total of 54 feet. Camping is not allowed at the falls, but picnic tables and grills are scattered around the base of each plunge, where you can swim, picnic, and enjoy an afternoon. Animals are allowed but must be on a leash.

Best Time to Visit: The best time to hike is between May and October.

Pass/Permit/Fees: There is no fee to visit.

Closest City or Town: Farmington

Physical Address:
Small Falls
Main Street
West Central Franklin, ME 04970

GPS Coordinates: 44.85897° N, 70.51673° W

Did You Know? Hikers can visit a bonus waterfall, Chandler Mill Falls, by heading straight after the footbridge at the first waterfall.

America's First Mile

The first mile of U.S. Route 1 starts at Fort Kent, Maine. Head south on the paved trail that leads to the Dube House, precisely 1 mile from the historical marker. The Dube House was built in 1840 and is the oldest home in Fort Kent. America's First Mile Trail takes you through the historic Aroostook County. There will be markers for the Aroostook War and Fort Kent along the path. You will pass the post office, the library, and Monument Square before crossing the Fish River and reaching Dube House. The Fort Kent Train Station Museum and America's First Mile End Point are also open for tours at the end of the trail. If you want to continue hiking after visiting the museums, the trail connects with Fish River Greenway trails and other loops in Fort Kent.

Best Time to Visit: Walk the trail during the summer months between July and September.

Pass/Permit/Fees: It's free to walk America's First Mile, but museum entrance fees vary.

Closest City or Town: Fort Kent

Physical Address:
America's First Mile, U.S. Route 1
341 W. Main Street
Fort Kent, ME 04743

GPS Coordinates: 47.24942° N, 68.60185° W

Did You Know? From Fort Kent, U.S. Route 1 runs the entirety of the East Coast for a total of 2,369 miles down to Key West, Florida.

Bowdoin College Museum of Art

The collection of art on display at Bowdoin College Museum of Art is among the oldest in the country. The early collection started with 70 paintings and a portfolio of 140 drawings gifted by James Bowdoin III to the college. Today, art and artifacts from prehistoric to modern creatives are featured in the museum. The museum's antiquities collection showcases art from the Assyrian, Byzantine, and Roman empires, and guests can soothe their souls with over 8,000 sketches from the hands of Warhol, Picasso, Manet, and Rembrandt. In addition, the American collection features presidential portraits and works by Thomas Eakins and Rockwell Kent.

Best Time to Visit: Exhibits vary with the seasons, but the best time to visit is between Tuesday and Thursday. The museum is closed on Mondays.

Pass/Permit/Fees: Admission to the museum is always free.

Closest City or Town: Brunswick

Physical Address:
Bowdoin College Museum of Art
245 Maine Street
Brunswick, ME 04011

GPS Coordinates: 43.90826° N, 69.96595° W

Did You Know? The art has been on display at its current location in the Walker Art Building since 1894.

Bradbury Mountain State Park

Bradbury Mountain State Park trails are top rated for mountain biking, horseback riding, and cross-country skiing. Out of the six trails in the park, Tote Road is the best trail for cross-country skiing. Hike the short Terrace Trail to catch sight of the last remaining wine grapes growing on the terraces in the spring and summer months. The Summit Trail is the most popular in the park—it's the fastest path to the summit. However, the South Ridge Trail is narrower and steeper but less crowded and offers impressive views from its lookout. If you want to get closer to the wildlife, hit the Knight Woods Trail for interpretive panels describing nearby flora and fauna along the path.

Best Time to Visit: The best time to hike and camp is between August and October on a weekday morning to avoid crowds.

Pass/Permit/Fees: Daily admission is $4 for residents or $6 for nonresidents. Camping fees are $15 for residents and $25 for nonresidents.

Closest City or Town: Freeport

Physical Address:
Bradbury Mountain State Park
528 Hallowell Road
Pownal, ME 04069

GPS Coordinates: 43.89975° N, 70.17911° W

Did You Know? The park's Northern Loop Trail features a Cattle Pound, a fixture unique to Maine for corralling stray farm animals.

Freeport McDonald's

Step inside the original McMansion in Freeport, Maine, and decide for yourself if McDonald's cheeseburgers taste better when they're prepared inside an 18th-century Victorian house. This McDonald's restaurant was built in 1984 inside a 170-year-old home to adhere to the city's strict aesthetic guidelines.

Freeport was settled in the 1700s and has maintained much of its historic charm, something the golden arches would distract from. To accommodate, McDonald's changed their original design and purchased the Gore House, built in 1850 by wealthy local merchant named William Gore. The restaurant was later approved by the Freeport Historical Society and commended for its use of Italian and Greek Revival architecture.

Best Time to Visit: McDonald's is open year round, but the best time to visit is right after lunch.

Pass/Permit/Fees: Prices will vary by menu item.

Closest City or Town: Freeport

Physical Address:
McDonald's
11 Mallett Drive
Freeport, ME 04032

GPS Coordinates: 43.86099° N, 70.10161° W

Did You Know? This is the only McDonald's in Freeport, and it serves lobster rolls during the summer.

Desert of Maine

Land in Maine is unique, with a nutrient-rich layer of topsoil covering a sandy mixture of rock and sediment left behind from the glacial melt during the last ice age. Without this unique combination, the Desert of Maine would never exist. However, the Desert of Maine isn't actually a desert. The land was overused and overworked by improper farming and overgrazing until the topsoil was depleted. The glacial sand that remains swallowed farming equipment, buildings, and trees until it was abandoned in the early 20th century. Today, the desert has shrunk from 120 acres down to 20 as the grass, trees, and moss take back the land. A tram ride brings visitors around the perimeter of the desert, explaining its history and geology.

Best Time to Visit: Visit during October and November to avoid the crowds.

Pass/Permit/Fees: Admission is $16 for adults and $12 for children under the age of 12.

Closest City or Town: Freeport

Physical Address:
Desert of Maine
95 Desert Road
Freeport, ME 04032

GPS Coordinates: 43.86040° N, 70.15514° W

Did You Know? The types of farming practices that created the Desert of Maine also contributed to the Dust Bowl.

Saco River

Saco River is often referred to as "The River of Death" and is known to claim at least three lives every year by drowning. Legend tells of a curse placed on the river in the 17th century by Squando, chief of the Sokoki tribe, after three English sailors killed his infant son. The death ended the peace between the tribe and the settlers. But don't let the curse of Saco River deter you from swimming, kayaking, or tubing any length of this 135-mile river. The river itself is calm, and the most popular spot to float is near Swans Falls. Rafters and more experienced kayakers can brave the rapids near Steep Falls and Limington Rips. Campgrounds at Swan Falls and Woodland Acres are available year round, and visitors can rent boats, canoes, and kayaks in Fryeburg.

Best Time to Visit: Visit on weekdays during the summer when the river is as warm as bathwater.

Pass/Permit/Fees: It costs $15 per night to camp at Saco River.

Closest City or Town: Fryeburg

Physical Address:
Saco River Canoe & Kayak
1009 Main Street
Fryeburg, ME 04037

GPS Coordinates: 44.02857° N, 70.97322° W

Did You Know? Other versions of the Saco River curse tell how the chief's daughter, kidnapped by white settlers, fell out of their canoe and drowned in the Limington Rips.

Evans Notch

The Evans Notch Overlook provides sweeping views of the Saco and Androscoggin rivers from atop the White Mountains. The Blueberry Mountain Loop Trail just touches the New Hampshire border before leading hikers to the overlook. The 8-mile loop is a moderate hike, but the lake is a perfect spot to rest and have a picnic. However, there is more than one way to climb a mountain. You will have your choice when it comes to trails depending on which direction you head. Royce, East Royce, and Laughing Lion trails climb the Royce Mountains to the west, while the Bickford Brook and Spruce Hill trails lead to Speckled Mountain in the east. During the spring, Spruce Hill Trail (2.8 miles) and East Royce trail (3 miles) are your best chance for wildflowers. In the fall, veer off the Blueberry Mountain Loop to the Bickford Brook Trail (3 miles) into New Hampshire for the changing leaves.

Best Time to Visit: The best time to hike Evans Notch is between April and October.

Pass/Permit/Fees: It's free to hike Evans Notch.

Closest City or Town: Gorham

Physical Address:
Evans Notch Overlook
Highway 113
Chatham, ME 03813

GPS Coordinates: 44.29784° N, 70.99726° W

Did You Know? The White Mountains, including Evans Notch, is a portion of the famous Appalachian range.

Schoodic Point

Schoodic Point is the only part of Acadia National Park on Maine's mainland. Visitors can access the point via a one-way road that breaks off at the south to lead to Schoodic Point. Most people bring beach chairs to sit back and enjoy the views of the surf and Cadillac Mountains, but there are seven hiking trails and picnic areas with fire pits and more. To get to the top of Schoodic Head, follow the Anvil, East, or Schoodic Head trails. The Anvil trailhead starts 1 mile away at the Blueberry Hill Parking area, or you can take the Buck Cove Mountain Trail near the campgrounds in the Schoodic Woods to climb Buck Cove Mountain on your way to Schoodic Head. For an easier hike, take the Sundew Trail to the research center.

Best Time to Visit: The best time to visit and hike is between March and October.

Pass/Permit/Fees: It costs $15 per person or $30 per vehicle to visit Acadia National Park, and campgrounds cost between $22 and $60 per night.

Closest City or Town: Gouldsboro

Physical Address:
Schoodic Point
Arey Cove Road
Winter Harbor, ME 04693

GPS Coordinates: 44.33281° N, 68.06094° W

Did You Know? The Schoodic shoreline is formed by ancient volcanic activity that forced dark basalt through the granite rock.

Maine Wildlife Park

Maine Wildlife Park is less a zoo and more a wildlife reserve for injured, abandoned, and human-dependent animals. It features over 30 Maine species, including moose, foxes, hawks, and eagles. Visitors have opportunities to feed and get up close and personal with these animals. The visitor center provides many other hands-on activities as well. In addition, families are invited to hike and explore two nature trails in the park. One focuses on the different trees growing in Maine and features an outdoor classroom while the other encourages hikers to find hidden animals. During the spring, the three gardens at the park are in full bloom. You can walk the garden grounds, keeping an eye out for wildlife that make their home there.

Best Time to Visit: The park is only open from April to November.

Pass/Permit/Fees: Admission is $7.50 for seniors over 60 or children under 12, $10 for adults, and $5 for military personnel with ID.

Closest City or Town: Gray

Physical Address:
Maine Wildlife Park
56 Game Farm Road
Gray, ME 04039

GPS Coordinates: 43.92804° N, 70.34795° W

Did You Know? You are guaranteed to spot a moose, Maine's state animal, at the wildlife park.

Mount Kineo

Humans visit Mount Kineo for its breathtaking views and valuable natural resources. It is named for Kinneho, the legendary Wabanaki warrior, and native tribes used the mountain's rhyolite stone to make flints, arrowheads, and more. Mount Kineo still provides shelter for the peregrine falcons who returned to the area after nearing extinction.

Reaching the summit of Mount Kineo is relatively easy by way of an old fire warden's trail: Bridle Trail. More experienced hikers can choose the Indian Trail (0.9 miles) for a steep and quick trip to the top. To indulge in the scenery, take the North Trail (2 miles) through the southeastern cliffs or follow the Mount Kineo Loop (3.4 miles) across Moosehead Lake. If you plan on staying in nearby Greenville, don't miss a game of golf on the original 1893 Mount Kineo Golf Course.

Best Time to Visit: The best time to hike Mount Kineo is between April and May.

Pass/Permit/Fees: Day passes to the mountain are $3 for residents or $4 for nonresidents.

Closest City or Town: Greenville

Physical Address:
Mount Kineo State Park
Northwest Piscataquis, ME 04441

GPS Coordinates: 45.70252° N, 69.73360° W

Did You Know? Mount Kineo was used as the Maine Forest Fire Tower until 1960.

Bailey Island Bridge

It may not look like much, but the Bailey Island Bridge is one of the most reliable structures in Maine. It was built with a unique cribwork style to withstand Maine's sometimes violent winds and tides. The design allows the tide to ebb and flow freely under the bridge without disrupting the traffic above. The cribstone bridge came about out of necessity when the people of Bailey Island asked the town of Harpswell to build a bridge connecting them to nearby Orr's island. In 1928, the original Bailey Island Bridge was built with slabs of granite from a nearby quarry in Yarmouth. The granite was latticed together to create a unique feat of civil engineering that remains in use to this day. Bailey Island Bridge is one of 74 cribstone bridges in the country and earned its listing on the National Register of Historic Places in 1975.

Best Time to Visit: The best time to visit Bailey Island is between May and October.

Pass/Permit/Fees: It's free to visit and cross Bailey Island Bridge.

Closest City or Town: Harpswell

Physical Address:
Bailey Island Bridge
Harpswell Islands Road
Bailey Island, ME 04003

GPS Coordinates: 43.75007° N, 69.98858° W

Did You Know? The bridge was restored in 2010 using stones from the original quarry in Yarmouth.

Eagle Island State Historic Site

Eagle Island is home to famed north-pole explorer Robert Peary. Peary retired in 1911 after buying the island 30 years earlier. Today, the home is a National Historic Site, and visitors are welcome to explore the property and the island. Boat tours are available on the weekends, or you can take your own tour via the 1.4-mile trail system that winds through the island. Admiral's Way, the oldest trail, was carved by Peary himself and crosses the highest point on the island. Hikers can take Raspberry Loop through a blueberry patch to get to the trail. On the west side of the island, the Great Horned Owl Path leads through owl nesting grounds.

Best Time to Visit: Most trails are closed for nesting until mid-July, so the best time to visit is between August and October.

Pass/Permit/Fees: Resident admission is $4 for adults, $2 for seniors, and $1 for children. Nonresident admission is $6 per person. Boat tours start at $40 per person.

Closest City or Town: Harpswell

Physical Address:
Eagle Island State Historic Site
Eagle Island
Harpswell, ME 04079

GPS Coordinates: 43.71245° N, 70.05320° W

Did You Know? Peary built two circular bastions to protect the home during stormy weather and used one of the bastions to store artifacts from his expeditions.

Lily Bay State Park

Lily Bay State Park is the premier spot for waterfront camping. The park's 925 acres sit on the south shore of Moosehead Lake, the largest lake in the state. Boating, fishing, and swimming await summer campers, while visitors can ice fish, snowmobile, and cross-country ski in the winter. The 5-mile X-country Ski Loop Trail adds 2 miles with its side trails through the North Woods. The trail is moderate but has sharp turns where beginners should be cautious. In the summer, hikers can take the Shoreline Trail (2 miles) to soak in the views of Moosehead Lake and Mount Kineo. Lily Bay State Park is known for its wildlife sightings. If you want to see a moose, bear, or deer in the wild, then hiking in the state park is a must.

Best Time to Visit: The best time for fishing is between May and September, and the best time to camp is between June and August.

Pass/Permit/Fees: Resident admission is $4 for adults, $2 for seniors, and $1 for children. Nonresident admission is $6 per person.

Closest City or Town: Jackman

Physical Address:
Lily Bay State Park
425 Lily Bay Road
Beaver Cove, ME 04441

GPS Coordinates: 45.57057° N, 69.55139° W

Did You Know? Moosehead Lake reaches a maximum depth of 246 feet.

Beals Island

Beals Island is true to the maritime history of Maine. It's the best place to catch lobster boats at work on the Bold Coast Byway. If you plan to stay a few days, get a lesson in maritime research on a tour of the Downeast Institute and hike a trail (or three) at the Great Wass Island Preserve. Hiking on the preserve is strenuous, especially in wetter weather, but casual hikes are best during low tide. Bring your binoculars on the out-and-back Mud Hole Trail (2.6 miles) and keep an eye out for wildlife. More experienced hikers can take the Telephone Line Trail (3.9 miles) along the coast. The tiny, picturesque town of Beals on the island can be reached by bridge from the neighboring island town of Jonesport. The population is around 500, and it hosts an art gallery, gift shops, and a handful of inns and restaurants.

Best Time to Visit: The best time to visit and hike is between April and September.

Pass/Permit/Fees: It's free to visit Beals Island, and overnight stays in Jonesport average between $100 and $300 per night.

Closest City or Town: Jonesport

Physical Address:
Beals Island
Washington County
Beals, ME 04611

GPS Coordinates: 44.51428° N, 67.61048° W

Did You Know? Each year, the people of Beals light the world's tallest lobster-trap Christmas tree.

St. Anthony's Franciscan Monastery

Escape for a meditative moment of solitude at St. Anthony's Franciscan Monastery. Shrines and chapels are tucked into quiet corners throughout the grounds, and visitors are welcome from sunrise to sunset. Overnight stays are available at the guest house from May to December. The monastery's walking trail begins in the guest house parking lot. The paved path loops through a wooded area and back around to the guest house, and there are unpaved trails through the woods for guests to explore. A guide to the shrines and chapels on the trail is available at the gift shop. Visitors must wear long sleeves and long pants or skirts, and women must wear scarves.

Best Time to Visit: The monastery is open year round with daily mass at 7:30 a.m. on weekends and 8:00 a.m. on the weekends. There is also an evening service at 7:00 p.m. on Wednesdays and Fridays.

Pass/Permit/Fees: It's free to visit the monastery. Overnight stays cost $99 to $259 for single rooms or $139 to $289 for group rooms.

Closest City or Town: Kennebunk

Physical Address:
Franciscan Monastery
28 Beach Avenue
Kennebunk, ME 04043

GPS Coordinates: 43.35538° N, 70.47801° W

Did You Know? The Olmsted Brothers designed the monastery's landscaping.

68

Goose Rocks Beach

Goose Rocks Beach offers a true-to-the-coast experience with nothing commercial on the island except a general store, a restaurant, and two hotels. In addition, there are seven beachfront properties owned by the Kennebunkport Trust available for rent during the summer. The 3-mile beach is perfect for families, with tide pools at low tide for kids of all ages to play and find wildlife.

Animal lovers will enjoy birdwatching in the area, and you can sometimes find harbor seals sunning themselves on the shore. Most of the beach is protected by the Rachel Carson Wildlife Refuge. Nearby Dock Square offers up art galleries, ice cream parlors, and fine dining for tourists year round. Visitors can also book boat excursions or play a round on any of the three golf courses on the island.

Best Time to Visit: The beach will be crowded during the summer, so visit during late August into September.

Pass/Permit/Fees: It's free to visit Goose Rocks Beach.

Closest City or Town: Kennebunkport

Physical Address:
Goose Rocks Beach Association
19 Community House Road
Kennebunkport, ME 04046

GPS Coordinates: 43.42334° N, 70.41730° W

Did You Know? There is no food, drink, restrooms, or changing areas at the beach, but you can find what you need at the general store or the Tides restaurant.

Kennebunkport

The coastal town of Kennebunkport incorporates Cape Porpoise, Ocean Avenue, Dock Square, and Lower Village. During the summer, the town celebrates the weeklong Kennebunkport Festival with local vendors, fine dining, and wine tastings. Fall and winter feature special holiday events, and local inns offer seasonal packages for visitors looking to stay awhile. Kennebunkport still operates as a fishing town, so hang around the marina to see lobstermen with their catch of the day. For a closer look at the history of Kennebunkport, head to the Seashore Trolley Museum. As the largest electric railway museum in the world, it offers a unique perspective into the history of public transport in Maine and the country overall. Then, hop on a trolley for a ride to the Smith Preserve hiking trails.

Best Time to Visit: The best time to visit is between September and December to avoid the summer crowd.

Pass/Permit/Fees: The average cost of a hotel in Kennebunkport is between $100 and $200 per night.

Closest City or Town: Kennebunk

Physical Address:
First Families Kennebunkport Museum
8 Maine Street
Kennebunkport, ME 04046

GPS Coordinates: 43.38083° N, 70.45194° W

Did You Know? The area was devastated by the Great Fire of 1947, a forest fire that destroyed over 17,000 acres.

Mother's Beach (Kennebunk Beach)

Mother's Beach is one of the three beaches that make up the coast of Beach Avenue. Kennebunk Beach earned the name Mother's Beach for being a family-friendly coast among Maine's rough and rocky shoreline. The sandy beach is protected by large rock formations on either side, with soft white sand and a playground on the western side. Stroll Mother's Beach along the sidewalk by the seawall or follow it for 1.5 miles through nearby Gooch's and Middle beaches. Middle Beach is the rockiest of the bunch, so make sure you bring shoes if you plan to walk the length of the shore. Dogs are allowed on the beach, and guests are encouraged to picnic as there are no concessions or food trucks. Surfing is also permitted at the beach.

Best Time to Visit: Visit when lifeguards are on duty from June through September.

Pass/Permit/Fees: Mother's Beach is free, but nonresidents must pay $25 for a parking pass.

Closest City or Town: Kennebunk

Physical Address:
Mother's Beach
263-267 Beach Avenue
Kennebunk, ME 04043

GPS Coordinates: 43.34421° N, 70.49888° W

Did You Know? The traditional beach houses have gold tiles on their roofs that weather and turn gray.

Ocean Avenue

To really see the rocky Atlantic coast of Maine, you have to drive Ocean Avenue. The 2-mile stretch along the coast is known for its ethereal sunsets and crowded marinas packed with sailboats, fishing boats, and yachts. There are very few stopping points, so drive slowly to capture the moment and be aware of stopping cars and pedestrians. The historic St. Ann's Episcopal Church sits along Ocean Avenue where it was built in 1887. The church has free parking and picnic spots.

Take advantage of nearby trolley tours or the historic inns if you plan to stay along the coast. Drivers can extend the ride by following Ocean Avenue to Turbat's Creek Road. From there, you can drive through Wildes District Road, lined with historic, custom-made homes, and onto Maine Street through the historic district of Kennebunk.

Best Time to Visit: There is much less traffic between March and April.

Pass/Permit/Fees: It's free to drive Ocean Avenue, but the cost to stay per night can vary.

Closest City or Town: Kennebunk

Physical Address:
Ocean Avenue
Kennebunkport, ME 04046

GPS Coordinates: 43.34228° N, 70.46731° W

Did You Know? The average price for a home on Ocean Avenue is $1.5 million.

Parsons Beach

Parsons Beach is a privately owned piece of coast tucked away just past the Rachel Carson Trail. The crescent-shaped beach is small, quiet, and beautiful. The Parson family has owned the beach for generations, and they leave it open from sunrise to sunset for visitors. If you visit during the summer, you can expect a crowd. Vacation rentals are available on the beach and nearby. Follow rural Parson's Road to reach the beach, but be respectful. Camping, fires, parties, and surfing are not allowed. Vehicles are also not allowed on the beach, and parking is scarce. You may want to bike or hike from the 1-mile Carson Trail in the Rachel Carson National Wildlife Refuge. You can hop on the trail at the refuge's parking lot.

Best Time to Visit: Visit during winter to avoid the crowds, or come in May and September for swimming.

Pass/Permit/Fees: It's free to visit Parsons Beach.

Closest City or Town: Kennebunk

Physical Address:
Parsons Beach
Parsons Beach Road
Kennebunk, ME 04043

GPS Coordinates: 43.34429° N, 70.51827° W

Did You Know? An 18-foot beaked whale, one of the rarest whale species, washed up on Parsons Beach in 2003.

Walker's Point Estate

Visitors can't actually tour Walker's Point Estate, but it is still worth the visit. Park your car at the turnout near Blowing Cave Park to take some pictures, then hop back in to drive past for a closer look. Former President George H. W. Bush inherited the property from his grandfather, who purchased the land in the 1870s. The Bush family continues to vacation here, and the presidents have hosted the likes of Margaret Thatcher, and Colin Powell. While you can get close enough to the property to see the grounds from your vehicle or by bike, remember that Secret Service is always patrolling the area. Exercise caution and drive safely.

Best Time to Visit: Visit between March and May or during the winter to avoid the traffic and crowds.

Pass/Permit/Fees: It's free to see the compound on Ocean Avenue drive.

Closest City or Town: Kennebunk

Physical Address:
Blowing Cave Park
208 Ocean Avenue
Kennebunkport, ME 04046

GPS Coordinates: 43.341717° N, 70.467827° W

Did You Know? If the Bush family is at home, the American and Texas flags at the house will be waving.

Wedding Cake House

Out of all the beautiful and historic homes in Maine, the Wedding Cake House is the most popular. It was built in 1825 by the Bourne family and given to their son, sea captain George W. Bourne, as a wedding gift. The Gothic-style buttresses and intricate woodwork were added by the captain later after he was inspired by the cathedrals in Spain. George Bourne was not just a captain but also a master carpenter and shipbuilder. He constructed the new barn and carriage house in the Gothic style after a fire in 1852. He then hand carved the lacy Gothic designs and pinnacles added to the rest of the home throughout his life. Drive or walk down Summer Street to get photos of the house, surrounded by a wrought-iron fence.

Best Time to Visit: Visit the home in April or May.

Pass/Permit/Fees: It's always free to drive by and take photos of the home, but tour prices can vary by event.

Closest City or Town: Kennebunk

Physical Address:
Wedding Cake House
104 Summer Street
Kennebunk, ME 04043

GPS Coordinates: 43.38242° N, 70.51698° W

Did You Know? Captain George W. Bourne built everything entirely on his own but asked for help once from a shipbuilder's apprentice named Thomas Durrell.

Basilica of Saints Peter and Paul

The Basilica of Saints Peter and Paul in Lewiston, Maine is not only one of the largest churches in New England but also one of the most well-known. There was a strong presence of Roman Catholic French Canadians during the early 20th century, partially due to tensions between the United States, Britain, and France. Many people settled in Lewiston to work the mills. In 1857, the Portland diocese sent a French-speaking priest to hold services. By the 1900s, the church had grown to the point of needing a larger facility, which led to plans being drawn up for the Basilica of Saints Peter and Paul. In 1983, the church was added to the National Register of Historic Places.

Best Time to Visit: The Basilica is accessible year round, but you may only enter on Sundays and during special events.

Pass/Permit/Fees: It's free to enter for services or events.

Closest City or Town: Lewiston

Physical Address:
Basilica of Saints Peter and Paul
122 Ash Street
Lewiston, ME 04240

GPS Coordinates: 44.09876° N, 70.21242° W

Did You Know? The church is known for its two pipe organs made by Casavant Frères and dedicated in 1938. One is located above the sanctuary and the other in the gallery. Both organs are electro-pneumatic action.

Devil's Footprint

The source of one of Maine's spookiest ghost stories sits just west of I-95—The Devil's Footprint. As the story goes, the construction of Scribner Road was deterred by an immovable boulder. After too many unsuccessful attempts at removing the rock, a worker exclaimed that he would sell his soul to Satan to have it moved. The next morning, the rock was mysteriously moved to its current location in the cemetery wall, and the worker was never seen again. The rock tells the tale of the missing man. There are imprints of a cloven hoof and a footprint that imply the man was chased by the Devil. Visit the cemetery at the North Manchester Meeting House Church to decide for yourself. The Devil's footprint is located to the right of the church, about a minute's walk through the cemetery, as part of the stone wall surrounding the property.

Best Time to Visit: Visit the church in late May for mild weather and fewer crowds.

Pass/Permit/Fees: It's free to visit.

Closest City or Town: Manchester

Physical Address:
North Manchester Meeting House Church
143 Scribner Road
Manchester, ME 04351

GPS Coordinates: 44.35755° N, 69.86359° W

Did You Know? Visitors often report seeing visions of a ghostly man with a lantern guarding the cemetery's gate.

Mount Katahdin

Mount Katahdin is the highest point in Maine and the final point on the Appalachian Trail. The most popular path to the summit is 9 miles long, starting with the Helen Taylor Trail from the Roaring Brook Campground parking lot. Hikers can also reach the summit from the Abol (Abol Trail), Katahdin Stream (Hunt Trail), or Chimney Pond (Cathedral Trail) campgrounds. Different trails lead to different sites on your way to the peak, and reservations are required ahead of time for each hiker. The Helen Taylor Trail takes you to Pamola Peak but adds another 5 miles to the hike. If you follow the trailheads from Chimney Pond Campground, you'll get views of Chimney Pond Lake along the way. Grab a map from Baxter State Park to decide which trail is best for you.

Best Time to Visit: The best time to hike to the peak is between March and October.

Pass/Permit/Fees: It's free for Maine residents, but out-of-state visitors must pay $12 per vehicle to enter the state park.

Closest City or Town: Medway

Physical Address:
Mount Katahdin
Northeast Piscataquis, ME 04462

GPS Coordinates: 45.90526° N, 68.92710° W

Did You Know? Mount Katahdin's summit reaches 5,267 feet tall.

Pockwockamus Rock

One of the first things you will notice on a trip to Baxter State Park is the mural on Pockwockamus Rock. With the peak of Mount Katahdin rising in the background, the wildlife scene urges everyone who sees it to "Keep Maine Beautiful." Pockwockamus Rock is a flat-faced boulder near the entrance of the state park and the Penobscot Outdoor Center. The flat surface inspired many graffiti artists to create their own works of art, but some childish profanity became an eyesore, and a group of teenage conservationists designed a mural in 1979 to preserve the rock and the park. The idea for the wilderness scene was meant to deter future graffiti and inspire visitors to appreciate and protect the natural beauty of Maine. Today, Pockwockamus Rock is a migratory point for naturalists and adventurous alike.

Best Time to Visit: Avoid the crowds by seeing the rock in late spring or early fall.

Pass/Permit/Fees: Admission to Baxter State Park is free for residents or $12 per vehicle for nonresidents.

Closest City or Town: Medway

Physical Address:
Pockwockamus Rock
135 Basecamp Road
Millinocket, ME 04462

GPS Coordinates: 45.79690° N, 68.88263° W

Did You Know? Originally, conservationists just wanted to paint a solid block of color over the graffiti.

St. Croix River

The historic St. Croix River travels along Maine's border with New Brunswick. It played a significant role in the War of 1812 and became a hotspot for the illegal lumber trade in the mid-19th century. Today, visitors can canoe the river to various campgrounds along the shore, where they can camp, fish for trout and salmon, birdwatch, and more. Guided canoe tours are available, with day and overnight trips that include all supplies and meals, but visitors are allowed to explore the river on their own as well. The St. Croix River system is a Y-shaped branch, with the West Branch showcasing Grand Lake and the American side, and the East Branch showcasing Spednic Lake and the Canadian side. The branches meet at Grand Falls Flowage, and experienced explorers can enjoy some mild white-water canoeing.

Best Time to Visit: The best time to camp and canoe the river is in the summer.

Pass/Permit/Fees: It's free to camp. Guided canoe tours can cost between $400 and $900 for a 3-day trip.

Closest City or Town: Medway

Physical Address:
St. Croix River, Vanceboro Railway Bridge
Public Crossing Road
Vanceboro, ME 04491

GPS Coordinates: 45.11488° N, 67.09930° W

Did You Know? The river's tide can rise and fall 25 feet in some spots.

Asticou Azalea Garden

If you visit Acadia National Park, be sure to visit Asticou Azalea Garden at Mount Desert Island. The tranquil oasis is tucked away on Route 3 and welcomes visitors with curated pathways through a Japanese-inspired garden of native Maine and Japanese plants. The garden pathways lead to nooks and crannies made of trees and blooms. Snuggle in and sit on the stone benches to listen to the birds sing, or stroll further down the path to soak in the aroma of azaleas, rhododendrons, and lilies. Depending on when you visit, you will see different blooms. Come in early May for the Japanese cherry blossoms or see Maine's native azalea bloom in June. Water lilies bloom in August, and the garden is alight with changing leaves in September and August. For more beautiful blooms, visitors can take a 15-minute walk to the nearby Thuya Gardens.

Best Time to Visit: The garden is only open from May 5 to October 31.

Pass/Permit/Fees: It's free to visit, but a $5 donation is encouraged.

Closest City or Town: Mount Desert

Physical Address:
Asticou Azalea Garden
3 Sound Drive
Northeast Harbor, ME 04662

GPS Coordinates: 44.30688° N, 68.28381° W

Did You Know? Volunteers regularly rake the garden paths to make them look like flowing water.

Somesville Museum and Gardens

Somesville was the first village settled by Europeans on Mount Desert Island in Somes Sound. Today, the town is registered as a National Historic District and preserves some of the earliest examples of early New England architecture. Somesville Museum and Gardens represents the town's history and is surrounded by blooms planted at the turn of the century. The museum also features the village's iconic white footbridge, which crosses the pond. Museum exhibits change every summer and feature tidbits of Somesville and Mount Desert Island history. But the garden is the museum's most impressive artifact, and visitors can take advantage of different educational opportunities offered throughout the season. Herbs and seeds from the museum's garden are also available in the gift shop.

Best Time to Visit: The museum is open from June to September.

Pass/Permit/Fees: It's free, but donations are encouraged.

Closest City or Town: Mount Desert

Physical Address:
Somesville Museum and Gardens
2 Oak Hill Road
Mountt Desert, ME 04660

GPS Coordinates: 44.36284° N, 68.33490° W

Did You Know? Somesville is actually named for its second settler, Abraham Somes, and not Governor James Richardson, whose family arrived first.

Pondicherry Park

Pondicherry Park is in the heart of downtown Bridgton. Hike the 3 miles of trails, including the accessible Kneeland Spring Trail (0.2 miles), which leads you to a historic spring, or explore the whole park on Pondicherry Loop Trail (1.2 miles), which spans Steven's Brook.

You'll cross a beautiful, covered bridge over Steven's Brook and another at the entrance of the park. The Bob Dunning Memorial Bridge at the park's entrance was constructed in the traditional barn-raising style. Across the park's 66 acres, visitors will also find picnic spots and an educational amphitheater that is sometimes used as an outdoor classroom by nearby Steven's Brook Elementary. Camping is not allowed, and bikes are not permitted on hiking trails. Pets are allowed but must be kept on a leash.

Best Time to Visit: The park is open year round but is very crowded on the weekends, so visit during the week.

Pass/Permit/Fees: It's free to visit Pondicherry Park.

Closest City or Town: Naples

Physical Address:
Pondicherry Park
Depot Street
Bridgton, ME 04009

GPS Coordinates: 44.05278° N, 70.70893° W

Did You Know? Kneeland Spring in Pondicherry Park never freezes because the water bubbles up from the bottom.

Sebago Lake State Park

Sebago Lake is the second-largest and deepest lake in Maine, reaching 316 feet at its lowest point. Its water is so clean that it's exempt from the state's drinking-water filtration requirements. The lake spans nearly 45 square miles, which means there's plenty of room for boaters, swimmers, kayakers, and canoers during the peak summer months. The Sebago Lake State Park public swimming area starts on the banks of the Crooked River, but there are many beaches and shores to lay down a blanket and soak up the coast. The state park campgrounds are to the east, and the historic Songo Lock Swing Bridge between the beach and the campsites is still in operation. From the beach, head south on Park Access Road to reach the Sebago State Park Trailhead.

Best Time to Visit: Visit the lake around Labor Day to avoid crowds.

Pass/Permit/Fees: Admission is $6 for residents and $8 for nonresidents to visit the lake.

Closest City or Town: Naples

Physical Address:
Sebago Lake State Park Swimming Beach
11 Park Access Road
Casco, ME 04015

GPS Coordinates: 43.98912° N, 70.69602° W

Did You Know? Two WWII Corsairs are at the bottom of the lake; they crashed during a training flight in 1944.

Shawnee Peak

Shawnee Peak Ski Resort features 245 acres with 19 trails lit for night skiing. Skiing started on the peak in 1935 and kicked off after WWII when the resort became the first in Maine to have a T-bar ski lift. The resort sits atop Pleasant Mountain, with a 1,900-foot summit and 1,350-foot vertical drop for the most adventurous skiers. Skilled skiers can also hit The Dungeons and the East Glades, two of the most popular double-black-diamond trails at the resort. Shawnee Peak is also an excellent spot for beginners. Lessons are available for all ages and skill levels, and beginner trails like the West Slope and Happiness 15 will get everyone comfortable in their skis. Overnight, all of the beginner trails are lit.

Best Time to Visit: The best time to ski is between November and February.

Pass/Permit/Fees: Lift tickets cost between $49 and $83 for a full day or $29 to $45 for night skiing. Ski rentals cost $57 for full-day use and $50 for night skiing.

Closest City or Town: Naples

Physical Address:
Shawnee Peak
119 Mountain Road
Bridgton, ME 04009

GPS Coordinates: 44.05900° N, 70.81520° W

Did You Know? The first ski trail at Shawnee Peak was the Wayshego Trail, which was carved into the mountain in 1935.

Songo River

Songo River is only 3 miles long but is one of the most historically important rivers in Maine. It flows from Long Lake, feeds into Lake Sebago, and holds the Songo Lock, the last 19th-century lock still in operation in Maine. The lock is mainly used today by visitors and tourists. Boats use it to reach Lake Sebago, one of the premier fishing spots in the state.

The Songo River is one of the busiest, especially during the summer when the water is dotted with kayaks, paddleboats, and River Queen tour boats. Take the Songo River Trail from Thompsons Point Road to hike to the river. You can also hop on the Songo Wilderness Trail from Thompsons Point, but this path will take you away from the river.

Best Time to Visit: Visit during the late spring or early fall months to avoid crowds.

Pass/Permit/Fees: Songo River is in Sebago State Park, which costs $6 for residents and $8 for nonresidents to enter.

Closest City or Town: Naples

Physical Address:
Songo River Queen II
841 Roosevelt Trail
Naples, ME 04055

GPS Coordinates: 43.97581° N, 70.60256° W

Did You Know? The Songo Lock raises and drops the water depth by an average of 5 feet.

Colonial Pemaquid State Historic Site

Pemaquid was home to the native Wabanaki tribe for 7 millennia and became one of the earliest colonized settlements in the United States. It was a melting pot of maritime life in the early 17th and 18th centuries. The site operated as a trading post until it became a permanent settlement in 1628. However, the site was attacked and abandoned twice before 1700 and was abandoned entirely by 1759. The ruins remained untouched until archaeological and historical interest piqued in 1903.

Today, visitors can explore the museum, pier, historical village, and reconstructed Fort William Henry, originally built in 1692. On the weekends, re-enactments of early settler life take place at the smithery and cottages on site.

Best Time to Visit: Visit from March to May to take advantage of the boat tours and day trips while avoiding the summer crowds.

Pass/Permit/Fees: It costs $3 for residents and $4 for nonresidents to visit the site.

Closest City or Town: New Harbor

Physical Address:
Colonial Pemaquid State Historic Site
Colonial Pemaquid Drive
New Harbor, ME 04554

GPS Coordinates: 43.87948° N, 69.52062° W

Did You Know? The cemetery on site is home to graves dating back to the 1620s.

Monhegan Island

Sneak away to Monhegan Island if you need a quiet escape. The tiny artist's island is a "walking island," barely a square mile across, and visitors' cars are not allowed in order to maintain its romantic charm over the centuries. What began as a lucrative trading post became an artist's colony in 1890. It hasn't changed much since then, with art galleries, restaurants, and inns on every corner that capture the beauty of coastal Maine. Take in the coastal views for yourself on the island's 9 miles of hiking trails. Lobster Cove Trail (0.5 miles) features wildflowers and birdwatching on its way to the shore, and Burnt Head Road Trail (0.5 miles) offers impressive views of the coast for hikers who aren't afraid to get wet. More experienced hikers can take the Whitehead Trail (1.5 miles) along the coast, but watch out for poison ivy.

Best Time to Visit: The best time to take the ferry over to the island is between April and October.

Pass/Permit/Fees: Round-trip ferry rides cost $42 for adults and $21 for children.

Closest City or Town: New Harbor

Physical Address:
Monhegan Museum
1 Light House Hill Road
Monhegan, ME 04852

GPS Coordinates: 43.77011° N, 69.31617° W

Did You Know? The local population of Monhegan Island was only 64 people during the 2020 census.

Battery Steele

Battery Steele is one of the many abandoned military batteries on Maine's coast. Initially constructed in 1942, it's the largest battery in the United States and once housed two 12-inch guns. The path there may be muddy, and you'll have to enter through a tunnel that is overgrown with grass, moss, and trees. However, there are miles of tunnels inside the battery that are decorated with street art from locals and tourists. In addition, secret events are hosted there throughout the year, and remnants of the parties linger behind. The entire site of Battery Steele spans 14 acres and includes the original gun emplacement, fire-control towers, and range-finding bunkers that face the sea. Hikers can reach the bunker via the Peaks Island Loop Trail (4 miles).

Best Time to Visit: Visit during the late summer or early fall when the weather is mild.

Pass/Permit/Fees: It's free to explore Battery Steele.

Closest City or Town: Peaks Island

Physical Address:
Battery Steele
Florida Avenue
Peaks Island, ME 04108

GPS Coordinates: 43.65785° N, 70.18116° W

Did You Know? The underground tunnels aren't lit, so bring a flashlight if you plan to explore the belly of the battery.

Quoddy Head State Park

Quoddy Head State Park is a naturalist's paradise, with five different hiking trails, rare habitats, whale watching, and more. Pack a picnic and visit for the day or take advantage of vacation rentals on the nearby beaches. To see a majority of the park, take the Coastal Trail Loop. The 4-mile trail is the most challenging but offers the best views of Gulliver's Hole, High Ledge, and the ocean leading into Canada. If you want to learn more about Quoddy's diverse flora, take the Inland Trail (0.75 miles) to the Bog Trail (1 mile), which features interpretive signs describing the moss, lichens, and other plants that grow in the unique climate of the park. The highlight of Quoddy Head is the peppermint-striped West Quoddy Head Light. The 19th-century lighthouse is closed to visitors, but the grounds are open.

Best Time to Visit: Quoddy Head is only open between May and October.

Pass/Permit/Fees: It costs $3 for residents or $4 for nonresidents to visit the park.

Closest City or Town: Pembroke

Physical Address:
Quoddy Head State Park
973 S. Lubec Road
Lubec, ME 04652

GPS Coordinates: 44.81652° N, 66.95288° W

Did You Know? The light produced by the West Quoddy Head Light still shines through its original 19th-century Fresnel lens.

Babb's Covered Bridge

Babb's Covered Bridge was originally one of the oldest covered bridges left in Maine. It linked the two cities of Gorham and Windham since it was first constructed in1864, but it was burned down by vandals in 1973. Fortunately, the historical societies in both cities worked together to rebuild it. Today, Babb's Covered Bridge is still open to traffic, but be aware of other vehicles as the bridge is one-way. You should also watch out for pedestrians who climb through a hole in the bridge's roof to jump into the river below. If you want to explore the area, leave your car behind and visit the bridge via the Presumpscot River. With limited parking, there aren't many opportunities to get out and explore by foot, so hop in a kayak or canoe for amazing views from under the bridge.

Best Time to Visit: The best time to visit is late August and early September when the weather is mild and the summer crowds are gone.

Pass/Permit/Fees: It's free to see and cross Babb's Covered Bridge.

Closest City or Town: Portland

Physical Address:
Babb's Covered Bridge
Hurricane Road
Gorham, ME 04038

GPS Coordinates: 43.76665° N, 70.44796° W

Did You Know? The rebuilt bridge was dedicated in 1976 as part of the U.S. Bicentennial celebration.

Casco Bay

Casco Bay is a series of islands that's home to some of Maine's largest and most iconic cities. A tour of Casco Bay will start to the south in Portland, the only mainland city in the bay. From there, you can choose to take a Casco Bay Line ferry or the Mailboat, which stops at five different islands on its hours-long journey. Each island at Casco Bay offers something different. Leave your car on the mainland and rent a bike on Peaks Island to explore the trails and Civil War memorials. Get in the water and kayak to Fort Gorges on Hog Island or pack your fishing pole for a trip to Long Island. There are 100 to 200 islands in Casco Bay, and it may be impossible to see them all. However, each will offer a fantastic view of the Gulf of Maine that borders two states and two Canadian provinces.

Best Time to Visit: The best time to visit Casco Bay is in the fall when the summer crowds have already left.

Pass/Permit/Fees: Ferry rides to the island range between $7 to $12 for adults and $3 to $6 for children or seniors.

Closest City or Town: Portland

Physical Address:
Casco Bay Lines Ferry Terminal
Maine State Pier
Portland, ME 04101

GPS Coordinates: 43.74205° N, 69.99880° W

Did You Know? The most populated island in Casco Bay is Peaks Island, whose population has tried to secede from Portland six times since 1883.

Fort Gorges

Fort Gorges was designed to support the American Civil War but did not reach completion until 1865 when the war was ending. By then, more modern weaponry made the fort obsolete, and the facility was never updated. It remains frozen in time as a testament to 19th-century American engineering. The short-lived Fort Gorges never saw battle, and soldiers were never stationed here. It was named a National Historic Landmark in 1973 and opened as a park where visitors can explore a unique piece of historical engineering. You can only access Fort Gorges by boat, and visitors are encouraged to kayak or canoe to the landmark. Guided historical tours are also available that lead guests through the officers' quarters, magazine, and parade grounds. Guests can also see one of the oldest Union artifacts from the Civil War—a 300-pound Parrott rifle.

Best Time to Visit: Summer and early fall are the best times to visit Fort Gorges.

Pass/Permit/Fees: It's free to explore Fort Gorges.

Closest City or Town: Portland

Physical Address:
Friends of Fort Gorges
400 Congress Street #17834
Portland, ME 04112

GPS Coordinates: 43.65979° N, 70.25731° W

Did You Know? Though little used, Fort Gorge did play a role in WWII when it stored submarine mines.

Fort Williams Park

Pack a picnic and enjoy the ocean views at Fort Williams Park. Amenities include tennis courts, beaches, hiking trails, historic sites, and a lighthouse. Listen out for the foghorn from Portland Head Light on overcast days when it warns sailors of the shore. The Ship Cove beach is on the north side of the shore. At low tide, you can walk the tiny beach and soak in the sight of the Ram Island Ledge Light in Casco Bay across the way. Just north of Ship Cove are Battery Keyes and the Goddard Mansion. Follow the Fort Williams Park Loop (0.8 mi) to circle the lighthouse and reach Ship Cove. From there, follow Shore Road to get to the battery and mansion. Along the way, you can stop for lobster rolls, gelato, or grab a sandwich from the three local restaurants in the park.

Best Time to Visit: The best time to hike is in the summer, but you'll enjoy a quiet serenity if you visit in winter.

Pass/Permit/Fees: It costs $2 per adult and $1 per child to visit the park.

Closest City or Town: Portland

Physical Address:
Fort Williams Park
1000 Shore Road
Cape Elizabeth, ME 04107

GPS Coordinates: 43.62234° N, 70.21198° W

Did You Know? George Washington ordered the construction of the Portland Head Light at Fort Williams.

International Cryptozoology Museum

Get your Bigfoot fix at the International Cryptozoology Museum in Portland. Cryptozoology is the study of hidden and unknown animals that are referred to as cryptids. This includes discovered species such as the coelacanth and megamouth shark and still-hidden species like Loch Ness and BigFoot. Cryptid displays feature specimens and replicas of famous creatures, including an 8.5-foot-tall Crookston BigFoot, Santa Claus's family tree, and strange paintings by the museum's owner, Loren Coleman. Other artifacts include famous hoaxes, including the P.T. Barnum "Feejee" Mermaid and the Civil War Pterodactyl. Visitors should not take the subject matter too seriously but rather consider the timelines of extinct or thought-to-be extinct creatures throughout history and how that continues to shape the lore and legends over the centuries.

Best Time to Visit: The best time to visit the museum is between April and May.

Pass/Permit/Fees: Admission is $10 for adults and $5 for children.

Closest City or Town: Portland

Physical Address:
International Cryptozoology Museum
32 Resurgam Place
Portland, ME 04102

GPS Coordinates: 43.65225° N, 70.29069° W

Did You Know? The museum was named the 7th-weirdest museum in the world by *Time* magazine.

Long Lake

One visit to Maine and you'll quickly learn there are many "Long Lakes" and "Long Ponds" scattered throughout the state. However, only one 11-mile Long Lake in Southern Maine connects the quiet towns of Naples and Bridgton to Harrison. Stop for a picnic at Long Lake Park in Harrison or catch a ride on the water at any nearby marinas. A short 5-minute drive around the lake will lead you into Bridgton and the Lakeside Pines Campground, which is open year-round. The Pondicherry Park and Stevens Brook Trailheads are also nearby. If you want to hike to Long Lake, take the Stevens Brook Trail from Highland Lake in Bridgton. Long Lake is the second-largest freshwater lake in Maine. If you want to stay lakeside for the summer, book ahead so that you don't miss your chance.

Best Time to Visit: Long Lake is always crowded during the summer months, so visit in late August or September.

Pass/Permit/Fees: It's free to visit the parks around the lake, but marinas and campgrounds will have a fee. Campsites at Long Lake are between $54 to $75 per night.

Closest City or Town: Portland

Physical Address:
Long Lake Park
Main Street
Harrison, ME 04040

GPS Coordinates: 44.12181° N, 70.68304° W

Did You Know? Long Lake is the origin of the mysterious mist in Stephen King's thriller *The Mist*.

Maine Narrow Gauge Railroad Museum

While the museum itself is a small, short tour, the real gem of the Maine Narrow Gauge Railroad Museum is the preserved train track. Take a ride on any of the museum's restored train cars, from a vintage caboose to old steam engines, and enjoy the waterfront views of Casco Bay. Don't hesitate to ask docents and train conductors questions about the history of Portland and the trains. The museum offers a unique look at the city that many have forgotten, and it features family-friendly events on the holidays from October through December. If you want to see more train cars than the restored cars on the ride, take a short road trip north to Alna. The city is an hour away but home to the Wiscasset, Waterville, & Farmington Railway Museum, which features many of the train cars once on display in the Portland location.

Best Time to Visit: The museum is open from April 1 until October 31, but events onboard vary year round.

Pass/Permit/Fees: Entrance fees are $12 for adults, $10 for seniors, and $6 for children.

Closest City or Town: Portland

Physical Address:
Maine Narrow Gauge Railroad
49 Thames Street
Portland, ME 04101

GPS Coordinates: 43.66096° N, 70.24645° W

Did You Know? Maine's narrow gauge is 2 feet wide, which is half the U.S. standard for rail tracks.

Peaks Island

Peaks Island is a quaint day trip from Portland, and the ferry conveniently runs every 15–20 minutes. Rent a golf cart or a bike to explore the island when the weather is nice. See most of the island on Peaks Island Loop (4 miles) from the western coast to the east and back again. Between a few delicious local restaurants and beautiful views of the coast, Peaks Island is a quiet getaway. Pop into the Fifth Maine Museum for a bit of history about the island, or stop by any of the art galleries. Local restaurants boast warm cinnamon rolls and ocean views, but leave room for ice cream. Two public beaches on the island are open year round, but only Sandy Beach is swimmable. At low tide, you can walk the shore and swim to nearby Catnip Island. Cairn Beach is a rocky beach best used for birdwatching, and you'll spy a few lighthouses from the coast.

Best Time to Visit: Avoid the island in the summer and come between April and May or September and October.

Pass/Permit/Fees: Ferry rides from Portland cost $8 for adults and $4 for children or seniors.

Closest City or Town: Portland

Physical Address:
Casco Bay Lines
56 Commercial Street
Portland, ME 04101

GPS Coordinates: 43.65765° N, 70.24868° W

Did You Know? During the summer, the population of Peaks Island surges from around 900 up to 4,000 people.

Portland Museum of Art

The Portland Museum of Art holds the most extensive collection of Western European art in Maine. Masterpieces by Degas, Magritte, and Monet are featured among the over 22,000 pieces in the museum. Works also highlight American artists, including impressionist Childe Hassam and illustrator N.C. Wyeth. Along with 18th- and 19th-century art, the museum hosts contemporary exhibits that alternate with the season. These exhibits feature local artists as well as creatives from across the globe. Past exhibits have included Bauhaus artists from Germany and single pieces by up-and-coming painters. The most popular spot in the museum is the sculpture park. The space is open to anyone during museum hours, and guests can pack a picnic and explore the grounds.

Best Time to Visit: Visit during the spring to get the most out of the sculpture garden without the summer crowds.

Pass/Permit/Fees: Admission is $25 for adults and $22 for seniors or students. Children ages 17 and under are free. Admission is free for all on Fridays.

Closest City or Town: Portland

Physical Address:
Portland Museum of Art
7 Congress Square
Portland, ME 04101

GPS Coordinates: 43.65470° N, 70.26248° W

Did You Know? An average of 140,000 people visit the Portland Museum of Art every year.

The Portland Observatory

Climb to the top of the Portland Observatory for a beautiful view of the city and the coast. The tower was originally built in 1807 to alert merchants and other important citizens to when their cargo would arrive. It stands 222 feet above sea level and was capable of seeing ships 30 miles from shore with its telescope. The observatory remained in use until the invention of the two-way radio in 1923.

It was declared a National Historic Landmark in 2006. The observatory is open seasonally for tours, and the grounds are open year round to visitors. The museum inside shows maritime artifacts from the 19th and 20th centuries and the flags used to alert different merchants. Each flag features a unique logo designed by the vessel owners.

Best Time to Visit: Tours inside the observatory are only available Thursday through Monday from July 1 to October 11.

Pass/Permit/Fees: Entrance fees are $10 per person.

Closest City or Town: Portland

Physical Address:
Portland Observatory
138 Congress Street
Portland, ME 04101

GPS Coordinates: 43.66614° N, 70.24837° W

Did You Know? Merchants paid an annual subscription fee of $5 to use the Portland Observatory.

Victoria Mansion

The Morse-Libby Home, also known as the Victoria Mansion, stands as a pristine example of early American architecture. The mansion was designed by Henry Austin with wall paintings by Guiseppe Guidicini. The home has maintained most of its decor and furnishings since 1893. Victoria Mansion was one of the first homes in Portland to feature hot running water, flushing toilets, and central heating. The museum showcases preserved appliances and light fixtures, and visitors are welcome to tour with docents or on their own. Plan your visit around any of the mansion's annual events, including a story time on the front lawn for families and afternoon teas with docents for adults who want to learn more about the museum.

Best Time to Visit: The museum is only open from May through December.

Pass/Permit/Fees: Admission fees are $16 for adults, $14 for seniors, $7 for students, and $5 for children. Families of up to six people can pay $35 for group entry.

Closest City or Town: Portland

Physical Address:
Victoria Mansion
109 Danforth Street
Portland, ME 04101

GPS Coordinates: 43.65221° N, 70.26074° W

Did You Know? The mansion was almost sold to an oil company and demolished to become a gas station during the Great Depression.

Maine Solar System Model

You might never make it into space in your lifetime, but you can still drive through the solar system on Presque Isle. Local technical and high school students constructed a 1:93,000,000 scale model of our solar system, starting with the sun at the Northern Maine Museum of Science. The model stretches down Route 1, with scale models of our neighboring planets at each of their relative distances.

The university recently received a grant to restore and promote the model, and it's been extended to feature three dwarf planets. Start your tour at the science museum and head south on Route 1. You'll spot Venus at the Central Aroostook Chamber of Commerce and Saturn in Westfield. The model ends with Pluto at the Houlton Information Center, precisely 40 miles from the science museum.

Best Time to Visit: Visit during late spring or early summer when the weather is best for photos.

Pass/Permit/Fees: It's free to drive through the solar system.

Closest City or Town: Presque Isle

Physical Address:
Solar System Model: The Sun
Folsom Hall
Presque Isle, ME 04769

GPS Coordinates: 46.67336° N, 68.01681° W

Did You Know? All of the planets are visible from the road except for Pluto.

Beech Hill Preserve

The view from atop Beech Hill will make you feel like you're in the Norwegian Highlands; the road and structures were all designed by a Norwegian immigrant in 1913. The hut at the top, built as a summer picnic home for a local family, is preserved as close to its original condition as possible.

Start your hike at the Beech Hill Preserve trailhead on Rockville Street. The 2-mile trail leads up the hill to the hut and back, giving visitors a chance to tour the woods, meadows, and grasslands surrounding the property. The summit of the hill stands 533 feet high, and you can walk around and through the historic stone hut for 360-degree views of the mountains and sea. A commercial blueberry farm is nearby.

Best Time to Visit: Hike the trail during early spring or late fall to avoid the crowds.

Pass/Permit/Fees: It's free to hike Beech Hill.

Closest City or Town: Rockport

Physical Address:
Beech Hill Preserve Trail Head
76 Rockville Street
Rockport, ME 04856

GPS Coordinates: 44.16174° N, 69.09430° W

Did You Know? The Coastal Mountain Land Trust acquired the land in 2003 and is preserving it as an organic blueberry and wildlife habitat.

Farnsworth Art Museum

The Farnsworth Art Museum features many of Maine's most influential painters, with four galleries devoted to modern artists from Maine and the rest of the world. One of the most famous paintings is Andrew Wyeth's *Christina's World*, and the museum also showcases the nation's largest sculpture collection from Louise Nevelson.

The museum is dedicated to preserving Maine's influence on American art. It was established by Lucy Farnsworth, the daughter of one of Rockland's oldest families. She used her inheritance to establish the museum, which also owns the original family home at 21 Elm Street. Take your time exploring the 20,000 square feet of gallery space.

Best Time to Visit: Avoid the crowds and visit between January and March. The museum is open from Wednesday through Sunday during the winter.

Pass/Permit/Fees: Entrance fees are $15 for adults, $13 for seniors, and $10 for students. Children ages 16 and under are free.

Closest City or Town: Rockland

Physical Address:
Farnsworth Art Museum
16 Museum Street
Rockland, ME 04841

GPS Coordinates: 44.10408° N, 69.10927° W

Did You Know? The museum was designed and built by local architects from Portland.

Rockport Marine Park

Rockport was once a busy harbor town. Today, it is one of the quietest spots on the coast, and the harbor is filled with pleasure boats and fishers. Rockport Marine Park is the perfect day trip, or you can choose the Timberwind cruises for a 4-day trip up and down the coast. If you stay on land, bring your tackle box and head for the dock. Enjoy a picnic at any of the tables or benches or lay out a blanket on the grass to soak up the iconic views of a 19th-century harbor practically frozen in time. Don't miss the antique kilns from when the harbor town was a thriving limestone quarry or the statute of Andre the Seal. Andre was discovered as a pup by the harbormaster in 1961 and stuck around to perform tricks and visit with tourists. He was sent to the aquarium in Boston every winter but would swim back up north to Rockport every spring until his death.

Best Time to Visit: Visit the park between May and September for the best weather.

Pass/Permit/Fees: It's free to visit the park.

Closest City or Town: Rockport

Physical Address:
Rockport Marine Park
Pascal Avenue
Rockport, ME 04856

GPS Coordinates: 44.18625° N, 69.07407° W

Did You Know? Andre the Seal unveiled his own sculpture at the park in 1978.

Ferry Beach State Park

Ferry Beach State Park features a picnic beach amid 1.7 miles of hiking trails and sandy white beaches. If you're hiking in August, look out for birds and wildlife snacking on the wild blueberries. Then, cross under Route 9 for a quick swim in the Atlantic. Ferry Beach is home to ten unique ecosystems, and the trails explore bogs, dunes, mixed forests, and more. The forest edge features rare Tupelo trees, and the nature center in the park offers visitors more information about the flora and fauna that reside here. Take the Tupelo Trail (0.4 miles) through the stand of Tupelo trees and cross the swamp on a raised boardwalk or follow the short Greenbriar or Witchhazel Trails (both 0.1 miles) through the hemlock forest.

Best Time to Visit: The beach is open seasonally from June to September, but you can still hike and cross-country ski the trails in the winter.

Pass/Permit/Fees: Admission is $5 for residents or $7 for nonresidents.

Closest City or Town: Saco

Physical Address:
Ferry Beach State Park
95 Bayview Road
Saco, ME 04072

GPS Coordinates: 43.47942° N, 70.38984° W

Did You Know? When highways did not yet extend north of Boston, travelers would ferry to the island, which is how the beach earned its name.

Higgins Beach

For a true summer getaway, escape to Higgins Beach. The tiny coastal village boasts only 300 homes and two inns, The Breakers and Higgins Beach Inn, which are only open in the summer. With very little parking at the beach, booking an overnight stay is better than planning an afternoon. The beach is well-known as a family area, with spots for picnicking, fishing, kayaking, and surfing.

During low tide, the shore is dotted with tide pools. Visitors might spot signs of the shipwrecks buried beneath the sand. Higgins Beach is also a popular spot for surfers. The ocean is relatively calm, but surfers will catch waves in all kinds of weather when it isn't. In addition, small beach communities mean fewer crowds, which gives Higgins Beach a lot more room for summer sports.

Best Time to Visit: Soak up the sun in the summer or visit the beach to catch waves in the winter.

Pass/Permit/Fees: The beach is free to visit, and rooms at the inns are between $160 to $200 per night.

Closest City or Town: Scarborough

Physical Address:
Higgins Beach Public Parking
20-40 Bayview Avenue
Scarborough, ME 04074

GPS Coordinates: 43.56183° N, 70.27658° W

Did You Know? Sixteen piping plovers, featured in Disney's animated short *Piper*, call Higgins Beach home.

Lenny the Chocolate Moose

Lenny is the only life-sized moose made entirely out of chocolate. Get a taste of some fresh chocolate—and a photo with Lenny—at Len Libby Candy Shop in Scarborough. The chocolatiers also sell ice cream and an assortment of homemade candies. It took 1 month and 1,700 pounds of chocolate to make Lenny. Even his pond is made out of chocolate. He was sculpted on site in 1997 and continues to greet guests at the entrance. The gift shop features huggable versions of Lenny and other chocolate creations in the shop, as well as games, recipe books, and more. If the warm aroma of chocolate and fudge doesn't entice you, stick around for some saltwater taffy or sour gummies. You can also taste some local Maine maple candies or sweet blueberries.

Best Time to Visit: The candy shop is open year round every day except Sunday.

Pass/Permit/Fees: It's free to see Lenny, but candies start at $3.

Closest City or Town: Scarborough

Physical Address:
Len Libby Candies
419 US-1
Scarborough, ME 04074

GPS Coordinates: 43.58418° N, 70.36364° W

Did You Know? Sculptor Zdeno Mayercak used the stuffed moose at the L.L. Bean in Freeport as inspiration for Lenny.

Old Orchard Beach

Old Orchard Beach has something for everyone. First, stroll the boardwalk to the pier for games, gambling, and food. Mini golf and go-karts are nearby, or you can visit Palace Playland for a ride on the Ferris wheel. Then, hit the sand for a castle-building competition or catch a wave with a surf or boogie board. At 7 miles in length, Old Orchard stretches over three towns, giving visitors a full taste of Maine coastal living. For a quieter vibe, visit Ocean Park, a Christian retreat tucked into the woodsy area of the beach. Old Orchard Beach has been a tourist resort since 1837 and was once able to have planes land and take off from its shores. Palace Playland hosted the country's first carousel and just built its latest metal coaster—The Sea Viper—in 2019, proving that fun has no age limit.

Best Time to Visit: The pier comes to life during the summer.

Pass/Permit/Fees: It's free to visit the beach, but it can cost between $5 to $20 to park.

Closest City or Town: Scarborough

Physical Address:
Old Orchard Beach Historical Society
4 Portland Avenue
Old Orchard Beach, ME 04064

GPS Coordinates: 43.52311° N, 70.37663° W

Did You Know? Palace Playland is the last old beach-based amusement park in New England.

Pine Point Beach

Pine Point is your kayaking destination, although it's likely more crowded than nearby Old Orchard Beach. However, there's plenty of beach to share. So, bring a picnic blanket as well as your surfboard, kayak, or fishing pole. Don't forget to bring a few dollars for the concession stand, too. If you want more than a snack, venture a few miles southwest for some delicious local seafood. More local restaurants line the road to the beach. On your way, you'll pass Snowberry Ocean View Park, a quiet spot to sit, walk, or rest while soaking up views of Maine's Atlantic coastline. Public beach access is available at Avenue 5. Visitors can rent kayaks, paddleboats, and beach bikes from a facility a quarter mile from the public parking lot. If you're on foot or bike, a trip to the beach is free.

Best Time to Visit: The beach is open for swimming from May through September.

Pass/Permit/Fees: It's free to visit the beach, and limited free parking is available. It costs $15 to park in the entrance lot ($35 for RVs).

Closest City or Town: Scarborough

Physical Address:
Pine Point Beach Public Parking
30-26 Avenue 5
Scarborough, ME 04074

GPS Coordinates: 43.54147° N, 70.33830° W

Did You Know? Pine Point Beach is a nesting ground for endangered piping plover birds.

Scarborough Beach State Park

The best beach in Maine features the warmest water. Summer swimming temperatures at Scarborough Beach State Park can reach the high 60s, making it a popular destination. Parking lots fill up before noon, so if you plan on taking a dip, arrive early. Set up a spot on the beach or explore via the 2-mile Scarborough Marsh Trail. It travels the length of the shore and is the perfect opportunity for birdwatching. You'll see the whole ecosystem working together in the state park. Swimmers be warned that rip currents are very powerful in this area, but lifeguards are on duty, and water conditions are clearly posted every day.

Best Time to Visit: Ocean temperatures are in the high 60s between July and August, but the best time to visit is between April and July.

Pass/Permit/Fees: For residents, day passes are $7 for adults and $5 for children. Nonresident admission is $9 and $6, respectively.

Closest City or Town: Scarborough

Physical Address:
Scarborough Beach State Park
418 Black Point Road
Scarborough, ME 04074

GPS Coordinates: 43.54685° N, 70.31300° W

Did You Know? The water in the area and surrounding Scarborough powered over a dozen sawmills in the 18th century.

Penobscot Narrows Bridge and Observatory

This bridge links the cities of Prospect and Verona together across the Penobscot River using a modern cradle system. The design doesn't require anchorages, leaving the view unobstructed, and visitors can climb to the top of the 420-foot-high observatory tower to take it all in. The view from the observatory is a 360-degree panoramic spectacle that sweeps across the river, the countryside, and historic Fort Knox. The observatory's entrance is designed to honor the historical landmark and features the same granite from a local quarry in Deer Isle. Interpretive markers throughout the area describe the historical significance of the river and Prospect's granite industry.

Best Time to Visit: The observatory and nearby Fort Knox are only open from May to October.

Pass/Permit/Fees: For residents, admission is $7 for adults and $2.50 for children or seniors. Nonresident admission is $9 and $5, respectively.

Closest City or Town: Stockton Springs

Physical Address:
Penobscot Narrows Bridge Observatory
740 Fort Knox Road
Prospect, ME 04981

GPS Coordinates: 44.56067° N, 68.80187° W

Did You Know? The Penobscot Narrows Bridge Observatory is taller than the Statue of Liberty.

Hurricane Island Center for Science and Leadership

Hurricane Island specializes in education programs for students aged 11 to 18. The center's STEM (Science, Technology, Engineering, Math) programs encourage kids to apply their research and education in the real world. Past programs have included lobstering, rock climbing, stargazing, and sculpture. Daily programs are available, making Hurricane Island the perfect day trip, but most programs last 2 to 12 days, with summer camps being the most popular stays for families. In the summer, the island opens up to the public for tours. You can reach Hurricane Island by boat or ferry. Cars are allowed on the island, but parking is limited. Catch the ferry from Rockland or set sail in your own vessel and dock at Journey's End Marina.

Best Time to Visit: Programs are available for students year round, but tourists can visit from June through August.

Pass/Permit/Fees: Mooring fees on the island are $15 per day and $25 for overnight stays. Public parking prices vary.

Closest City or Town: Thomaston

Physical Address:
Hurricane Island Center for Science and Leadership
19 Commercial Street
Rockland, ME 04841

GPS Coordinates: 44.10452° N, 69.10450° W

Did You Know? The summer camps and most of the facilities on Hurricane Island use sustainable practices.

Long Cove Quarry

Long Cove Quarry is one of the best swimming holes in Maine. Swimmers and street artists dive into the quarry from the cliff above all summer long. You may find a few visitors painting the rock face, and you're welcome to hike and climb nearby, but explore at your own risk.

No lifeguards are on duty, so be aware of your surroundings while swimming and lounging. Unfortunately, there is no beach, but swimmers can lay blankets on the rocks and grassy areas nearby.

Respect the quarry's "carry in/carry out" policy and do not leave any belongings or litter behind. The grounds are not maintained by the public and rely on the consideration of each visitor.

Best Time to Visit: The water in the quarry is warm enough for swimming in July and August.

Pass/Permit/Fees: It's free to swim at the quarry.

Closest City or Town: Thomaston

Physical Address:
Long Cove
Long Cove Road
St. George, ME 04860

GPS Coordinates: 43.99017° N, 69.20450° W

Did You Know? During the quarry's heyday, it employed immigrants from Sweden, Finland, and England.

Olson House

Visit the Olson House and climb into a 20th-century painting. The iconic farmhouse is featured in the famous painting *Christina's World* by Andrew Wyeth, a local artist whose family is well-known for their influence on 20th-century painting and illustration.

The farmhouse remains the same as it was when Wyeth painted it in 1948. It was initially built in the 1700s but was remodeled in 1871 when several rooms were added. Andrew Wyeth kept a studio in a room on the top floor but never owned the home. Instead, it belonged to his neighbors and lifelong friends, Christina and Alvaro Olson, with whom he spent many summers.

Best Time to Visit: The best time to visit is during late spring and early summer.

Pass/Permit/Fees: Entrance fees are $15 for adults, $13 for seniors, and $10 for students. Children ages 16 and under are free.

Closest City or Town: Thomaston

Physical Address:
Olson House
384 Hathorne Point Road
Cushing, ME 04563

GPS Coordinates: 43.98238° N, 69.26873° W

Did You Know? *Christina's World* is owned by the MOMA in New York City but displayed at the Farnsworth Art Museum in Rockland.

Owls Head Transportation Museum

Don't miss the annual auction at Owls Head Transportation Museum, hosted every August. Visitors will have the opportunity to see and bid on vintage vehicles like the 1959 Volkswagen Bus and 1986 Mack truck. Even if you don't win a bid, the museum itself is a prize. It features vintage vehicles dating back to the turn of the 19th century. Collections include the original Red Baron, a Phantom Rolls Royce, and a *Fads & Failures* exhibit with curiously designed vehicles from the past. Exclusive 3-D virtual experiences are new to the museum and provide visitors with an even closer look at some of the collection's most unique vehicles. Take the Melbourne Brindle experience for an almost hands-on look at the Rolls Royce.

Best Time to Visit: While the annual auction is in August, it's also a good time to visit in October or November.

Pass/Permit/Fees: Entrance fees are $14 for adults and $12 for seniors. Children under 17 and members of the military can visit for free.

Closest City or Town: Thomaston

Physical Address:
Owls Head Transportation Museum
117 Museum Street
Owls Head, ME 04854

GPS Coordinates: 44.06629° N, 69.10253° W

Did You Know? A Mercedes Benz built in 1885 is the oldest car in the collection.

Bass Harbor Head Lighthouse

The Bass Harbor Head Lighthouse in Acadia National Park was originally built in 1855 with a $5,000 grant from Congress. Now, it's actually a residence. A member of the Coast Guard and their family live there throughout the year, but visitors are welcome to explore the grounds and hike the trail nearby. Bass Harbor Head Light Trail is a short out-and-back hike around the grounds. Take in the scenic views and the coastal landscape, but the trail will be crowded during summer. Walk the path during low tide when you're able to climb across the rocks and photograph the lighthouse head on. It's one of the most-visited spots in the park, and sunset is the most popular time at the lighthouse. It will be near impossible to find parking if you arrive too late. The lighthouse stands 56 feet above the high-water mark, and it's a sight to see the waves crash on the rocks below it.

Best Time to Visit: Avoid the crowd and visit during March or April.

Pass/Permit/Fees: It's free to park and visit the lighthouse.

Closest City or Town: Tremont

Physical Address:
Bass Harbor Head Lighthouse
116 Lighthouse Road
Bass Harbor, ME 04653

GPS Coordinates: 44.22267° N, 68.33743° W

Did You Know? The lighthouse was featured on Maine's *America the Beautiful* quarter in 2012.

Charcuterie

The chefs at Charcuterie, an Amish deli in Unity, craft hand-ground meats the old-fashioned way. The store is lit by oil lamps and heated with a wood-burning stove. The meats are kept cold in an icehouse stocked with ice hand cut from the lake nearby every winter. Owner Matthew Secich was once a celebrity sous chef, managing five-star restaurants in some of the biggest cities in the country. He gave up the high-stress commercial kitchen environment for his Amish faith and a quiet lifestyle and can now be seen behind the counter with his wife and family. The menu boasts an array of cured and fresh meats, from kielbasa sausage to beef jerky. Flavors are also always changing, and you can try jalapeño, bacon, cranberry, and more.

Best Time to Visit: Charcuterie is open year round on Wednesdays, Fridays, and Saturdays.

Pass/Permit/Fees: Prices vary, and Charcuterie does not process credit or debit payments.

Closest City or Town: Unity

Physical Address:
Charcuterie
Leelyn Road
Unity, ME 04988

GPS Coordinates: 44.61372° N, 69.30711° W

Did You Know? Matthew Secich is most well-known for his tasting menus at Charlie Trotter's in Chicago.

Fawcett's Antique Toy and Art Museum

Fawcett's Museum is less a toy museum and more an art collection. Owner and curator John Fawcett has been collecting vintage toys and cartoon artifacts for 50 years. He earned a degree in graphic design and loves to discuss the history and cultural significance of his collection. Pop over to the gallery next door to see some of Fawcett's own works on display. Ironically, many of the items in the museum aren't meant for children. Instead, Fawcett wants visitors to consider the ways toys are used by both adults and children and how they shape the way we interact with the world. Some of the unique items in the collection include a bomb with Donald Duck's face on it, Betty Boop's pet dog Bimbo and discontinued boyfriend, and the original Lone Ranger paintings from WXYZ Radio.

Best Time to Visit: From Memorial Day to Columbus Day, hours are 10:00 a.m. to 3:00 p.m. with the museum closed Tuesday and Wednesday. From Columbus Day to Christmas, hours are 12:00 p.m. to 3:00 p.m. on weekends.

Pass/Permit/Fees: It's free to visit the museum.

Closest City or Town: Waldoboro

Physical Address:
Fawcett's Antique Toy and Art Museum
3468 Atlantic Highway
Waldoboro, ME 04572

GPS Coordinates: 44.60536° N, 69.249558° W

Did You Know? Some of the rarest items in the museum are a 1942 paper toy train and original *Snoopy* animation.

Matthews Museum of Maine Heritage

If you think you already know everything about colonial Maine, visit the Matthews Museum of Maine Heritage. With over 10,000 artifacts representing 18th-century life, you're bound to uncover something new. The agriculture museum welcomes visitors every summer to learn about the past and how it continues to impact Maine's future. When you enter the museum, you'll explore the traditional 18th-century town, with booths dedicated to blacksmithing, copper mining, cooking, weaving, and travel. In addition, local items from Union are displayed in the museum, including the original 35mm silent moving-picture camera from Union Town Hall. Matthews Museum is also often called the Moxie Bottle House for its extensive collection of Moxie memorabilia. Moxie is a regionally brewed soda drink, invented in Union, that is usually only recognized by New Englanders.

Best Time to Visit: The museum is only open in July and August.

Pass/Permit/Fees: It costs $4 to visit the museum.

Closest City or Town: Waldoboro

Physical Address:
Matthews Museum of Maine Heritage
1 Fairgrounds Lane
Union, ME 04862

GPS Coordinates: 44.21487° N, 69.28455° W

Did You Know? The Matthews Museum features one of two single-horse shay carriages left in existence.

Pemaquid Point Lighthouse

The Pemaquid Point Lighthouse was originally built in 1827 and commissioned by then-president John Quincy Adams. Today, visitors can climb the lighthouse, tour the inside, and visit the Pemaquid Art Gallery and Fishermen's Museum located on the premises. The lighthouse is still in operation and owned by the Coast Guard, but it's open seasonally for tours. Time your visit just right to climb to the top of the tower and take in the sweeping view of the sea. The museum hosts classes, concerts, movies, and other events throughout the year, so check the site calendar to plan ahead. Entrance fees to the park include access to the lighthouse, art gallery, museum, learning center, and picnic area.

Best Time to Visit: The lighthouse park is only open from May to October.

Pass/Permit/Fees: Entrance fees cost $3 per adult and $1 per child.

Closest City or Town: Waldoboro

Physical Address:
Pemaquid Point Lighthouse
1180 Bristol Road
Bristol, ME 04539

GPS Coordinates: 43.83693° N, 69.50606° W

Did You Know? The mortar for the original lighthouse was made with saltwater and started to deteriorate almost immediately. The lighthouse was repaired in 1835 with freshwater mortar mix.

Drakes Island Beach

Head down the southern coast of Maine if you're looking for long, sandy beaches. Drakes Island Beach offers a 2,800-foot beach with plenty of room for spreading out a blanket and soaking up the sun. Take a stroll on the shore or explore the rocky jetty that juts out from the beach. Water at Drakes Island is warmer than other parts of the coast, and beachcombers can explore tide pools during low tide year-round. During the summer, tourists and locals will crowd the parking lots, but the shore is wide open for a walk or nature hike in winter. Take the nearby Barrier Beach Trail for a 2-mile hike through the dunes and some birdwatching, or pick up bait on your way down and cast your line into the surf.

Best Time to Visit: The beach is open year round, but lifeguards are only on duty from May to September.

Pass/Permit/Fees: It's free to visit the beach, but parking will cost $4 for nonresidents.

Closest City or Town: Wells

Physical Address:
Drakes Island Beach
Island Beach Road
Wells, ME 04090

GPS Coordinates: 43.32429° N, 70.55145° W

Did You Know? Drakes Island Beach is a nesting area for the endangered piping plover, and posted signs will warn you to stay away from certain areas.

Ogunquit Beach

Ogunquit Beach is often voted as the best beach in New England for its soft sand, warm water, and gentle surf. The tiny coastal village of Ogunquit is well-known for its handmade fudge, chocolate, and ice cream. The soft sands stretch for 3.5 miles, and the heart of it is Footbridge Beach, which you access via a footbridge crossing the Ogunquit River. Here is where you'll find families building sandcastles or scavenging for seashells. Visitors can also access Main Beach from the town center or North Beach from Ocean Avenue. Lifeguards are on duty during the summer, but the beach remains open in the winter for fishing, hiking, whale watching, and more. In September, the beach hosts the Ogunquit Kite Festival as part of the weeklong Capriccio Festival that takes over the village every year.

Best Time to Visit: Visit after Labor Day between September and April for free parking.

Pass/Permit/Fees: Daily parking fees are $20 for Main Beach and $25 for Footbridge and North beaches.

Closest City or Town: Wells

Physical Address:
Ogunquit Beach Public Parking
115 Beach Street
Ogunquit, ME 03907

GPS Coordinates: 43.25593° N, -70.60047° W

Did You Know? *Ogunquit* is the Abenaki word for "beautiful place by the sea."

Ogunquit Museum of American Art

Maine is home to many famous American artists, and the Ogunquit Museum of American Art features the works of locals like Andrew Wyeth and Henry Strater. Henry Strater himself started the museum in 1953. Of the 3,000 permanent pieces in its collection, the museum is best known for housing Jack Levine's complete set of graphic works. Other famous artists featured in its most-recent exhibits are Philip Koch and Khalil G. Gibran.

Once you've explored inside, take a tour of the sculpture garden throughout the grounds of the museum. From here, you can watch the ships at Perkins Cove and enjoy the iconic Maine coastline that has inspired so many artists.

Best Time to Visit: The museum is only open from May through October.

Pass/Permit/Fees: Entrance fees are $12 per adult and $12 for students or seniors. Children 12 and younger can visit for free.

Closest City or Town: Wells

Physical Address:
Ogunquit Museum of American Art
543 Shore Road
Ogunquit, ME 03907

GPS Coordinates: 43.23437° N, 70.58917° W

Did You Know? The land where the museum stands was once home to a local art colony started by marine painter Charles Herbert Woodbury.

Perkins Cove

Perkins Cove is your next relaxing getaway. The tiny fishing village was originally an artist's colony, and exploring the coast may encourage you to pick up a paintbrush or visit a local art gallery. If the sea inspires you, take a lobster or fishing tour with one of the local fishing boats. Cocktail tours are also available, where guests are treated to dinner and views of the lighthouses. Stay aboard longer with a weeklong schooner cruise or book an extended stay on a houseboat. To explore the village on foot, take the Marginal Way trail along the coast. The 2.4-mile trail leads through town and along the water. Pick up the trailhead just past the Oarweed Restaurant.

Best Time to Visit: Plan your visit in May and June to avoid the bulk of the summer crowds.

Pass/Permit/Fees: The daily parking rate is $25, and nightly rates at local hotels are between $90 to $299.

Closest City or Town: Wells

Physical Address:
The Basin Dock
82 Perkins Cove Road
Ogunquit, ME 03907

GPS Coordinates: 43.23783° N, 70.59203° W

Did You Know? You may have the chance to operate the hand-operated footbridge in the village and raise it if a tall ship needs to pass through.

Eartha Globe

The largest rotating model of our planet Earth is right outside Portland. Designed in 1998 by David DeLorme, who affectionately refers to her as "Eartha," the globe sits over 41 feet wide, weighs nearly 5,600 pounds, and completes a full rotation every 18 minutes. Eartha Globe is designed on a scale of 1:1,000,000, where 1 inch equals 16 miles. She rotates on her axis in a 3-story glass building that is open seasonally for tours. Visitors can climb to the top level to see the highest parts of the globe. Although the gift shop and map store associated with Eartha are closed in the off hours, the globe continues to spin and remains illuminated every night. In addition, visitors can explore the geocaching display on the ground floor.

Best Time to Visit: The best time to see Eartha is early June or late August into September to avoid the crowds.

Pass/Permit/Fees: It's free to visit Eartha Globe.

Closest City or Town: Yarmouth

Physical Address:
Eartha Globe
DeLorme Drive
Yarmouth, ME 04096

GPS Coordinates: 43.80851° N, 70.16390° W

Did You Know? The state of California is 3 feet tall on Eartha Globe.

Boon Island Light

Boon Island Light is the tallest lighthouse in New England and sits on one of the tiniest islands off the Maine coast. Boon Island is only 300 by 700 feet but very dangerous. When the first ship ran aground in 1682, survivors were stranded on the island for a month. Then, in 1710, the shipwrecked crew of the *Nottingham Galley* had to resort to cannibalism while waiting to be rescued. Since then, the Boon Island Light risks all to guide sailors safely to shore. It was initially washed away in a storm in 1804 and again in 1832. Finally, when a blizzard in 1978 destroyed the lighthouse, the keeper's home, and other buildings on the island, the Coast Guard fully automated the outpost. Today, visitors can see the lighthouse from shore or venture into the sea for a closer look. Unfortunately, the lighthouse isn't open to the public, but you can access the island by boat.

Best Time to Visit: Visit during the summer when the weather is mild and the waters are calm.

Pass/Permit/Fees: It's free to see the lighthouse.

Closest City or Town: York

Physical Address: This lighthouse is remotely located on Boon Island off the coast of York. The only way to reach it is by boat or plane.

GPS Coordinates: 43.12185° N, 70.47592° W

Did You Know? Fishers and merchants would leave barrels of provisions on Boon Island in case of shipwrecks after the *Nottingham Galley.*

Cape Neddick Nubble Lighthouse

Cape Neddick Light—called "the Nubble" by locals—is likely the most famous lighthouse in Maine. It was one of the first lighthouses known to host public tours in the 19th century, and NASA included a digital image of the Nubble on the Voyager Golden Record. Today, while the lighthouse isn't open to the public, the city erected a park and swimming area to get visitors as close to Nubble Light as possible. Sohier Park features scuba diving, swimming, picnics, birdwatching, and fishing, with amazing views of the Nubble nearby. The Nubble Light is only 41 feet high but stands at 88 feet above sea level due to the height of the rocky jetty it sits on. After you snap the perfect photos, enjoy a picnic or grab a bite from the local lobster hut or ice cream parlor next door.

Best Time to Visit: The lighthouse is open seasonally from April to October.

Pass/Permit/Fees: It's free to visit the park.

Closest City or Town: York

Physical Address:
Nubble Lighthouse
Sohier Park Road
York, ME 03909

GPS Coordinates: 43.16605° N, 70.59140° W

Did You Know? Two former lighthouse keepers—William M. Brooks and William Richardson—were fired for ferrying tourists back and forth from the Nubble.

Cliff Walk

The Cliff Walk captures all the beauty of Maine in every season. Hike in spring for wonderful wildflowers along the trail or take a summer stroll and enjoy the mist from the waves. Fall and winter are the perfect months to enjoy the kind of cool solitude that can only be experienced on the coast. The 1 mile out-and-back trail is paved for most of the way as it snakes along the cliffs and rocky shoreline. Take in beautiful views of the water and stately homes of York Village. The path ends at a pebbled beach where you can search for sea glass before turning around and heading back. Pick up the Cliff Walk trailhead at York Harbor Beach and follow it along the coast. Bring a fishing pole if you have extra time.

Best Time to Visit: The best time to visit is between April and October, but the trail will be crowded in the summer.

Pass/Permit/Fees: It's free to walk the trail, but nearby parking prices vary.

Closest City or Town: York

Physical Address:
Cliff Walk
Harbor Beach Road
York, ME 03909

GPS Coordinates: 43.13298° N, 70.63873° W

Did You Know? Some of those wildflowers may be poison ivy, so be careful to stay on the path.

Fort Foster Park

Fort Foster Park welcomes visitors to swim and picnic on the historic grounds of Fort Foster, which was active between 1901 and 1945. The park is open daily with seasonal beaches, hiking trails, and a fishing pier. If you're traveling with pets, all beaches to the right of the pier are dog friendly.

While the park is crowded during the summer, with families on the beaches and picnics and weddings in the pavilions, spring and fall are the best time to hike the Kittery Point Shore Trail. The 2-mile loop touches the shore and leads hikers through the fort grounds. Visitors are allowed to explore, but the fort itself is closed except for the original Mine Control Station that serves as a public restroom.

Best Time to Visit: For hiking, visit between April and October. If you want to swim, visit in early June.

Pass/Permit/Fees: Admission is $20 per vehicle ($50 per RV).

Closest City or Town: York

Physical Address:
Fort Foster
Pocahontas Road
Kittery Point, ME 03905

GPS Coordinates: 43.07832° N, 70.69240° W

Did You Know? The fort's armaments were scrapped to support first WWI and then WWII.

Long Sands Beach

Long Sands Beach stretches for a mile and a half down the coast between York Harbor and York Beach. Southern Maine gets the warmest waters in the summer, and the beach will be crowded with umbrellas and blankets from June through September. There is no harbor, pier, or lighthouse to obstruct the water, so the waves are biggest at Long Sands. You'll find surfers in the water all year and families catching waves on boogie boards in the summer.

Parking is available nearby and up and down the neighboring streets. A trolley also runs between Long Sands, Short Sands, and York Beach, and it can be the best way to travel if you want to take in the view of the coast.

Best Time to Visit: Visit in September for the Labor Day festival or later in the month to avoid the crowds.

Pass/Permit/Fees: The public beach is free, but parking prices vary.

Closest City or Town: York

Physical Address:
Long Sands Beach
189 Long Beach Avenue
York, ME 03909

GPS Coordinates: 43.16094° N, 70.62105° W

Did You Know? At high tide, most of the beach is rocks and pebbles. Check the local tide chart before you head out.

Seapoint Beach

During the summer, the beaches in Kittery have the warmest water, including Seapoint Beach. However, the appeal of Seapoint isn't just the swimming. The primitive shoreline offers the best waterfront walking during the fall and winter. Seapoint Beach is pebbled and a perfect spot for finding sea glass. Keep an eye out as you stroll up the shoreline, but don't slip on the seaweed. If you're traveling with a pet, Seapoint Beach is one of the few Maine beaches that allows dogs during the summer season. Dogs are welcome year round (after 5 p.m. during the summer), so bring your leash and their favorite ball. For a more serious hike, venture to the Cutts Island Trailhead (1.8 miles) at the Rachel Carson Nature Preserve less than a mile from the beach.

Best Time to Visit: Between April and October is the best time to visit Seapoint Beach.

Pass/Permit/Fees: It's free to visit the beach, but parking prices can vary.

Closest City or Town: York

Physical Address:
Seapoint Beach
11 Seapoint Road
Kittery, ME 03905

GPS Coordinates: 43.09168° N, 70.66353° W

Did You Know? The best part of Seapoint Beach is seeing the beautiful views along Route 103 by car or bike.

Short Sands Beach

Short Sands Beach sits tucked between the rocky cliffs, right in view of the famous Nubble Lighthouse. Families can come for a picnic or swim or take a short stroll on the beach. The quarter mile of sand near Ellis Park is soft and white, but you will see the iconic rocky shores and colorful sea glass during low tide. Events happen seasonally at Short Sands, so plan your vacation accordingly. Fireworks pop over the water in July and August, and Ellis Park hosts nightly concerts all summer long. During the winter, the crowds disperse, and visitors can enjoy fishing and relaxing by the water. If you didn't bring a swimsuit, check out the playground and basketball courts nearby. Young children will love a trip to York Wild Kingdom at the beach. It's the largest zoo in Maine.

Best Time to Visit: Although it gets crowded, the summer months are the best time to visit Short Sands Beach

Pass/Permit/Fees: Parking at the beach is $2 per hour.

Closest City or Town: York

Physical Address:
Short Sands Beach
Hawk St
York, ME 03909

GPS Coordinates: 43.17430° N, 70.60759° W

Did You Know? The remains of a centuries-old shipwreck are buried in Short Sands Beach, and parts are often uncovered after strong storms and hurricanes.

Proper Planning

With this guide, you are well on your way to properly planning a marvelous adventure. When you plan your travels, you should become familiar with the area, save any maps to your phone for access without internet, and bring plenty of water—especially during the summer months. Depending on which adventure you choose, you will also want to bring snacks or even a lunch. For younger children, you should do your research and find destinations that best suit your family's needs. You should also plan when and where to get gas, local lodgings, and food. We've done our best to group these destinations based on nearby towns and cities to help make planning easier.

Dangerous Wildlife

There are several dangerous animals and insects you may encounter while hiking. With a good dose of caution and awareness, you can explore safely. Here are steps you can take to keep yourself and your loved ones safe from dangerous flora and fauna while exploring:

- Keep to the established trails.
- Do not look under rocks, leaves, or sticks.
- Keep hands and feet out of small crawl spaces, bushes, covered areas, or crevices.
- Wear long sleeves and pants to keep arms and legs protected.
- Keep your distance should you encounter any dangerous wildlife or plants.

Limited Cell Service

Do not rely on cell service for navigation or emergencies. Always have a map with you and let someone know where you are and how long you intend to be gone, just in case.

First Aid Information

Always travel with a first aid kit in case of emergencies.

Here are items you should be certain to include in your primary first aid kit:

- Nitrile gloves
- Blister care products
- Band-Aids in multiple sizes and waterproof type
- Ace wrap and athletic tape
- Alcohol wipes and antibiotic ointment
- Irrigation syringe
- Tweezers, nail clippers, trauma shears, safety pins
- Small zip-lock bags containing contaminated trash

It is recommended to also keep a secondary first aid kit, especially when hiking, for more serious injuries or medical emergencies. Items in this should include:

- Blood clotting sponges
- Sterile gauze pads
- Trauma pads

- Second-skin/burn treatment
- Triangular bandages/sling
- Butterfly strips
- Tincture of benzoin
- Medications (ibuprofen, acetaminophen, antihistamine, aspirin, etc.)
- Thermometer
- CPR mask
- Wilderness medicine handbook
- Antivenin

There is much more to explore, but this is a great start.

For information on all national parks, visit https://www.nps.gov/index.htm .

This site will give you information on up-to-date entrance fees and how to purchase a park pass for unlimited access to national and state parks. This site will also introduce you to all of the trails at each park.

Always check before you travel to destinations to make sure there are no closures. Some hiking trails close when there is heavy rain or snow in the area and other parks close parts of their land for the migration of wildlife. Attractions may change their hours or temporarily shut down for various reasons. Check the websites for the most up-to-date information.

Made in United States
North Haven, CT
12 December 2022

28611719R00085